RESEARCH CHALLENGES

Through the Use of the Atlas, the Almanac, and Other World Resources

Suggested curriculum, lessons, activities, and ideas for students* who want the doors to a world of knowledge opened to them.

by
Melissa Donovan

illustrated by Al Schneider

Cover by Judy Hierstein

Copyright © Good Apple, Inc., 1985

ISBN No. 0-86653-271-4

Printing No. 987654321

GOOD APPLE, INC.
BOX 299
CARTHAGE, IL 62321-0299

*The activities in this book were designed for gifted classes and field tested in such (grades four through eight). Most regular classes should find these activities enjoyable and beneficial also.

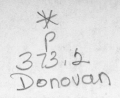
PREFACE

The total curriculum, lessons, activities, and ideas in this book have been designed for gifted students and field tested in classes for them. That is not to say that they would not be beneficial and enjoyable to most all students. Most of the criteria I used in planning this program for gifted students (see diagram on page vii in this book) should be used in all programs. Exceptions, of course, would be #3 and, for many students, #2. In some instances, some of the criteria may be of a more urgent need to gifted students if they are to actualize their potential. This will be discussed later.

I believe you can take any subject or topic and plan a curriculum for students around it using the criteria I've listed. I have chosen *reference books* (resources) as the subject and the *almanac*, *atlas*, and other *world resources* as the topics. Since *reference books* is a main criterion, I simply make it the main subject of my gifted curriculums. If students are taught through the books, about these books, how to use these books, and the value of these books, you will give them the key to a whole new world of knowledge. Gifted students, especially, should never have limits to the knowledge around them, so open doors to where it can be found.

However, it should be understood that it will take much more than simply placing these reference books into their hands. These books are only tools, and what we do with them will determine the extent of students' learning. To get students to the point of optimum learning, certain qualities have to be evident in the process.

The initial process begins with students wanting to do the lesson. All good teachers know more learning will take place if students are motivated to do it. It was my main challenge in designing these activities to create activities that were fun to do and also met all the learning objectives. If the lesson is challenging, it usually will be fun for a gifted child. Challenges are like games to gifted people; you become a winner if you can solve the challenge. For a lesson to be challenging, it should not repeat what is taught in the regular curriculum. Prior to designing the ideas in this book, I researched performance objectives of different school systems and then created a curriculum that is not normally taught. However, there may be a few concepts taught in this book that may be part of a regular curriculum's objectives, because they are prerequisites to more in-depth projects in this book.

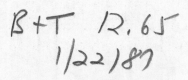

Most of the activities in this book are challenging because they demand higher level thinking skills from the students. Basically, *Research Challenges* introduces new information and skills to students and then asks them to use these in either higher level thinking activities or for in-depth projects.

A curriculum that stays motivating throughout and does not lend itself to boredom has to vary its activities as this curriculum does. From an atlas quiz bowl to a debate on which almanac is best, to helping a family from outer space cope with our ways, to helping Secret Agent 009 find his missing agents, to making a state collage—you should see your students curious and very motivated as to what new activity they will be receiving from this book next.

To aid the process of learning, let students find out for themselves. As you go through these activities in this book, hopefully you will notice that the teacher does little telling of facts, that students (in every case possible) are encouraged and led to find out for themselves. Questions that begin like "Can you find?" or "Can you think of?" are challenges in themselves to students who can find and who can think of. Why tell them if they can seek and find for themselves? The teacher takes the role of a facilitator in this book—to guide students in their process of learning. Besides finding information for themselves more challenging, students will also retain the information longer, and they will acquire confidence in seeking information on their own.

Students need to be given a purpose in doing an activity other than just being part of their school work. Most of the ideas in *Research Challenges* give the students purposes. Most all the information that is requested from the atlas, the almanac, and other world resources is for solving problems like 009's and the Maduhas' and for in-depth projects, such as the state collage, and for designing a school almanac.

In summary, most of the activities before you motivate, because they ask for the students' thinking skills and actions; they are unique from a general curriculum; they demand higher levels of thinking; and there is a purpose to each activity. Thus, the students should be motivated to pursue all activities.

This book and its activities offer to the teacher and students challenges in all the main academic areas besides teaching them about reference books. Most of the activities bring in many possibilities for inclusion of many of the academic areas in one lesson. If you can bring in more than one academic area to a lesson, you're going to multiply the students' learning and should whenever possible. The objectives prior to the activities state all the different things that the student will gain from each lesson.

The students will learn many facts in the academic area, but it is even more important they learn processes of how to do things. Once they learn certain processes, they will have new doors opened to all different areas. For example, how to debate can be used in all academic areas. How to do a simple art layout can be used whenever illustrations will add to a project, again in any subject. How to plan a school almanac should transfer over to all areas where planning will help something go more smoothly. How to do research correctly will be of benefit to the students the rest of their lives.

Of course, knowing facts and the process of how to do things won't do students any good later on in life if they can't work with other people. Bright students may often think their ideas are the best, and usually they are, but their ideas will never be actualized if they can't convince others of them. To convince others, you often need to relinquish part of your own ideas for theirs, instead of intimidating others by dogmatically insisting your ideas are the best. You have to listen to others and their ideas and find good in them, also. This whole process is a very difficult task that some bright people never accomplish, and because of it many of their bright ideas are never put into effect, and they become frustrated, unaccomplished human beings. This is a much more urgent need of gifted students than other students. This area should never be ignored when working with bright students. That is why most of the more in-depth projects in this book call for group involvement of sharing ideas, piggy backing ideas off one another, and sometimes demanding group concensus. There is a time and place for individualization (many of the ideas may be used as individualized activities), but we must remember bright people stimulate one another with their ideas, and also most people do not function totally alone successfully in our society anyway.

Let's face it. What is the underlying reason we teachers have been given the job to teach? It isn't for students to have fun or learn something everyday, though this is part of the process. It is to prepare students for their future. And I believe we should always ask ourselves with each lesson, "How are we doing that?" If we can answer it by an academic process and/or affective reason, then the activity is worthwhile. All the activities in *Research Challenges* purport to help students cope with their future. First of all, of course, if students are happy in the pursuit of these projects, they will be willing to make friends with the atlas, the almanac, and the other world resources taught, and it will hopefully be a key for them to further their knowledge anytime they want it—next week, next year, in college, on the job. Also, knowing how to find knowledge oneself instills a tremendous amount of self-confidence, initiation, and independence—all valuable skills that will be assets to those who hold them the rest of their lives.

Many of the projects in this book are quite involved and require many steps leading to the requested outcome. Again, I had the students' futures in mind when these activities were created. Bright students have the potential to become whatever they want to in the career world. Most successful careers, in one way or another, demand perseverance to accomplish many steps to achieve a long term goal. Students need this experience at an early age to develop that perseverance and also to feel the satisfaction and success of reaching the accomplished goal.

We, as teachers, can not assume bright students know how to do everything. Just like everyone else, they need to be shown how if they have never been taught before. Throughout this book I advocate, where possible, that the teacher shows an example of what is expected of the students (examples have been provided for you). Most of these activities should be unique to the students, and they will feel more confident in doing them if there is an example.

Taking into consideration the needs of gifted students in planning this book, hopefully you noticed the inclusion of consideration of the affective needs of these students. One of the biggest needs bright students have is they need to be challenged. If they're challenged, their minds are stimulated and utilized, and they are much more self-actualized people. This creates happiness, which should carry over to their personal lives. They may be very sensitive people with a need to help others. Many of the simulated activities give them this chance. Many are extreme perfectionists and will only attempt something if assured of the results. As was mentioned, student examples of what is expected are included in this book. Also step-by-step instruction is given, so there should be no questions on the how to.

The biggest area in which affective needs will be met is by working with others. Teamwork has to be accomplished in most cases before the final goal of the lesson can be achieved. I don't feel I can mention too often, when students become comfortable with using the atlas, almanac, other world resources, and other reference books, it will create confidence, self-initiative, and more independence.

Students need to make sense of a whole, especially gifted students, because they are always questioning the why's, the where's, and how everything fits into place. I have tried to lend continuity to this curriculum. All the lessons tie into one another which eventually leads to the total (whole) understanding of world resources. You have been provided with more than enough ideas for students to have total understanding of the atlas and the almanac and for them to have experience using all sections of them in fun, creative ways. The GUIDELINES section of this book will explain further how the activities relate to one another.

Everything posible has been put into this book to make the curriculum a success for the teacher and ultimately the students. The one ingredient I could not include was the teacher. It goes without saying, these ideas should be successful for you and your students if you are enthusiastic and that enthusiasm is carried over into the classroom while you are doing the activities with your students. I was always excited to try these ideas with my students, and their excitement as they progressed through the activities kept regenerating my excitement and thus theirs.

I hope you enjoy these activities with your students as much as I have with mine. I give you the key as you will give it to your students. I hope new and wonderful doors will be opened for you.

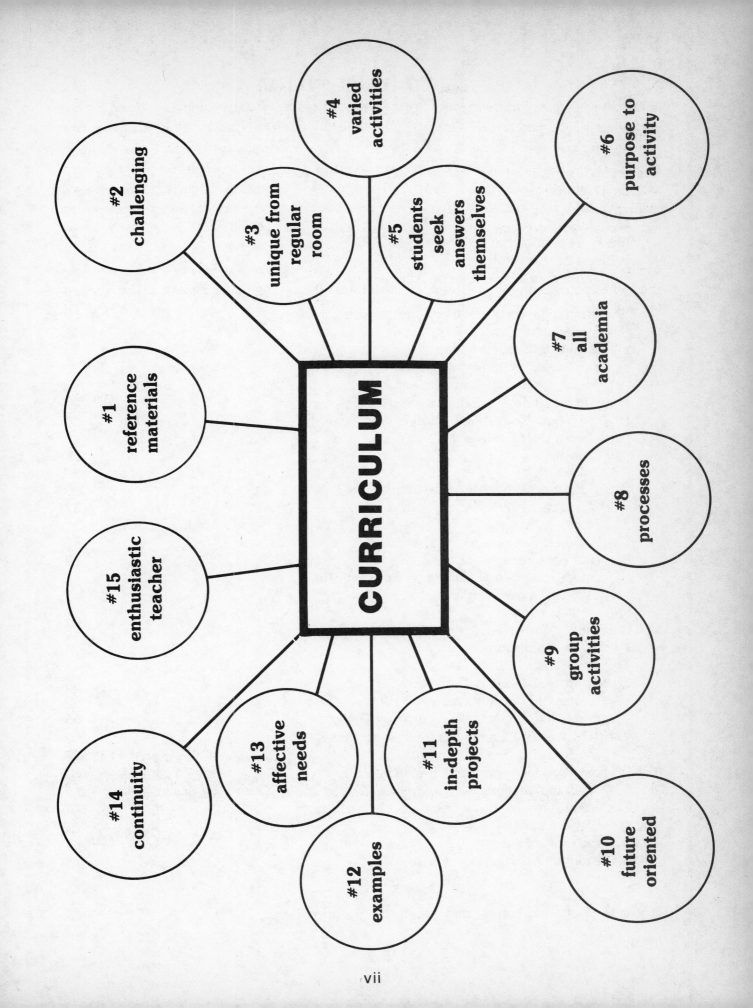

TABLE OF CONTENTS

*Definitions of mind bender and simulation are on page xii.

GUIDELINES

The four units of study in *Research Challenges* are on the atlas, the almanac, making a state collage using world resources, and other activities using world resources respectively. This book was designed to be used in an assortment of ways by the teacher. It may be used as total units of study, in which there are enough ideas for one year, or the teacher may choose one total unit for teaching, leaving the other three units for another time. If the teacher is going to teach only one unit, any of the four could be taught without teaching the others. However, if Unit III or Unit IV is chosen, keep in mind students should understand the basic concepts that are taught in Unit I. If the teacher chooses to do all four units, Unit III and Unit IV should be taught last, but it doesn't matter which of the other two are taught first.

Another way to use this book is to select various activities that interest you and your students and which fit into your own curriculum. Even though each activity adds to the total understanding of each unit, each may still be used alone where the teacher feels appropriate.

The underlying make-up and structure of each of the four units is somewhat different, because each requires different patterns of learning for total understanding of the main theme being taught. Because of this, the make-up and rationale of each unit will be discussed separately.

UNIT I   ATLAS

Understanding an atlas requires the interpretation of maps and various charts, which a number of the lessons in UNIT I help the student to do and thus need to be covered and understood before the student can handle some of the activities at the end of the unit. And you won't want to miss these activities (an atlas quiz bowl, a simulation, and a very challenging mind bender) because they are very highly motivating, educational, and fun.

You may choose to use "Do You Know Your Atlas?" on pages 24-25 in this book as a pretest to see if students know the prerequisite skills for these activities. You may choose to use it as a pretest anyway to determine what lessons you will teach in the unit.

UNIT II   ALMANAC

Of the four units, UNIT II has the most flexible structure, because getting the most use out of an almanac does not require prerequisite interpretation skills. It basically involves knowing what is in the almanac and how that information can be found. Becoming aware of everything housed in an almanac could prove a difficult task, because of an almanac's extreme quantity of words, statistics, and pages. However, it does not necessarily have to be a difficult task if you familiarize your students with sections of it with motivational activities which are provided in UNIT II. The unit has numerous activities and questions to pick from, and no sequential order has to be followed. However, the more activities you do, the more your students will know the almanac and benefit from it.

GUIDELINES—UNIT II ALMANAC

Teachers' manuals usually do not include teaching the almanac because the material becomes obsolete each year with each new, updated almanac. When it comes to specific questions asked of the students, make sure that they can be found in the three main almanacs and advocate using one or all of them: *The World Almanac and Book of Facts*, the *Reader's Digest Almanac and Yearbook*, and *Information Please Almanac*. There is no guarantee that every single answer will be in future almanacs, but the probability is there. As you will see, most of the activities in UNIT II allow for fluctuation in the make-up of the almanac.

UNIT III   STATE COLLAGE

When high school and college students are asked to use resources to find information for a project, it is customary to take notes on the information found, validate the information, and use this information in the final project. I wanted to design a project that would ask for these things of younger students so they would learn the correct process*, and at the same time keep them interested enough to want to pursue all the steps. I came up with the state collage.

Because there is a sequential process to research, some of the lessons in UNIT III have to be taught as such. However, there are still many ideas you may use in isolation of the rest of the unit, or ideas you may delete when pursuing the collage. Such ideas are the state fact categorizing game, drawing the collage true to scales, figuring out a light hook-up, and brainstorming symbols. However, these all add to make a beautiful and well-done collage.

UNIT IV

There are simply two main activities in UNIT IV: "Pen Pals" and "Travel Brochures." Students will have the opportunity with these two projects to use all kinds of world resources, especially the atlas and the almanac.

FORMAT OF THE LESSONS

The format of most of the lessons in this book is the same. The activity: the materials needed for it; its objectives; the directions of it; and personal comments from author are included with each lesson where needed. Student sheets with directions and examples are also provided. If they are specifically for the student, they are coded 🗝 . Teacher may want to also duplicate any correlated picture, at the beginning of activities, with student handouts.

Some of the student skill sheets in the ATLAS UNIT do not have directions preceding them, because the sheets are self-explanatory. For instance, most geography books cover longitude and latitude in the schools, so only a resource page for students to refer to prior to the game, "Where Am I?" is provided. The teacher will know if the resource sheet needs to be gone over or not with his or her student—it's there if it's needed.

Most answers to student assignments are found in the back of this book. However, a few follow the activity page if it is needed by the teacher to refer to in giving the lesson.

---

*Things that are normally taught with the research process such as a bibliography were avoided. These students should get instruction in this later in their regular curriculum.

STUDENT DICTIONARIES
(Suggestion for implementing with curriculum)

Students will be introduced to many new vocabulary words with the lessons in this book. I suggest having the students make their own dictionaries for these words. Students simply label twenty-six pages of paper from A to Z and put into a notebook. A three-ring notebook will work the best, because students may need to insert new pages.

As a word is given, the student inserts it in dictionary under the appropriate letter, underlines the word, writes its definition, and puts it into a sentence. When a page is filled up, student may number the words in alphabetical order.

Students should be allowed to insert new words of their own choosing, besides the ones the teacher gives. The dictionary will be the students' resource of new words, and the teacher will not have to keep repeating definitions.

Words below are used in this book, and students should become familiar with them if they aren't already. Other pages of words are incorporated into this book where the need arises.

brainstorm: to think of as many ideas as possible in certain amount of time

categorize: arrange things into groups with common characteristics

criteria: rules by which something is judged or evaluated; quality something has to have (criterion-singular form)

evaluate: to judge or review based on facts or criteria

mind bender: a challenging abstract situation in which critical and analytical thought processes can be organized so there are relations within the components.

simulation: a made-up, realistic situation in which problems have to be deciphered, criteria developed, and individual and group decisions made.

UNIT I
THE ATLAS

- Introduction
- WHERE AM I? (game)
- Sun/Earth relationship
- Measuring distance
- Figuring time around the world
- ATLAS TEAM QUIZ BOWL
- 009'S LOST SECRET AGENTS simulation
- CITY OF WORLD PEACE simulation

INTRODUCTION TO ATLAS

Activity: Student will look through an atlas or altases to determine all types of different information that can be found in it/them.

Material:
1. atlases (at least one for each student or pairs of students)
2. paper and pencils
3. dictionary (optional)
4. chalkboard

Objectives:
1. Student will familiarize himself with atlas(es).
2. Student will memorize types of information that can be found in an atlas for future reference.
3. Student will become interested in the use of an atlas.
4. Student will see the value of using an atlas.

Directions: Teacher makes atlases available to students.

Give students 15 to 20 minutes to become familiar with the atlases. At the end of the time period, have them close the atlases and write down as many different kinds of information as they can which they found. When students have exhausted their lists, come up with a group list. See the following page for possible answers. Have students open their atlases to see if they missed any answers.

As a **follow-up**, have class come up with a definition, of an atlas similar to the one below. Students may add to their dictionaries.

Atlas: a resource book of maps and other information about different places in the world.

As an **extension**, have students think up simple questions for one another to answer under each category on the following page.

Comments: Students can learn much more through this lesson (and have fun doing it) than if the teacher merely tells them the different types of information found in an atlas.

2

POSSIBLE THINGS YOU CAN FIND IN AN ATLAS

location of places: cities   continents   lakes
states   rivers   oceans
countries   seas   mountains

scales of miles

longitude and latitude lines

directions

time zones

world flags

air distances between major cities

longest river lengths

national park locations

facts on the solar system

average temperatures of places in the world

currency of places in the world

languages of places in the world

major occupations of places in the world

capitals of countries and states

square mileage of countries

population of countries

major ocean and sea areas

major mountain heights

major lake areas

number of county seats in state

facts on states

climate of places in the world

special/unique facts about places in the world

products of places in the world

topography* of places in the world

vegetation* of places in the world

*Definitions of *topography* and *vegetation* can be found on page 97.

WHERE AM I?

Activity: This is a game in which players apply their skills of latitude and longitude lines and directions to solve where the person (who is "it") is in the world.

Material:
1. Each player needs a map of the world: atlas insert, maps* from pages 8 and 9 in this book, or other map of the world.

2. Each player needs two pieces of paper or cardboard to mark off areas in which the person who is "it" is not in.

3. Person who is "it" needs a marker of some sort to locate on the map where he is.

4. Person who is "it" needs a make-shift stand to block map and marker from players' views.

Objectives:
1. Students will review longitude and latitude (resource page).
2. Students will review prime meridian and equator and apply knowledge.
3. Students will review directions of map and apply knowledge.
4. Students will understand the purpose of above concepts.
5. Students learn locations of many places in the world.

Directions: Person who is "it" finds a specific location on his world map which he wants the players to guess and places a marker there. Players ask questions leading to where the location is. Person who is "it" answers "yes" or "no."

Example of questioning process:
1. Are you an ocean? . . . . .no
2. Are you a continent? . . . . .no
3. Are you an island? . . . . yes
4. Are you south of the equator? . . . . .no
   (Players cover everything south with cardboard.)
5. Are you north of the equator? . . . . .yes
6. Are you west of the prime meridian? . . . . .yes
   (Players cover everything east with cardboard.)
7. Are you north of 20°N latitude? . . . . .yes
   (Players cover everything south.)
8. Are you north of 40°N latitude? . . . . .yes
   (More area is covered.)
9. Are you north of 60°N latitude? . . . . .yes
10. Are you north of 80°N latitude? . . . . .no

*If using pages 8 and 9, may want to place on tagboard and laminate for durability after maps are duplicated.

11. Are you between 60°N and 80°N? . . . . yes
12. Are you west of 60°W longitude? . . . . no
13. Are you between 60°W and 30°W? . . . . no
14. Are you between 0° and 30°W? . . . . yes
15. Are you Iceland? . . . . yes

If only two players are playing, then keep track of points/number of questions it takes to get answer. After so many times each has a turn, the one with the least points is the winner. This makes it more challenging for the person who is "it" to think of a difficult place to guess.

If more than two players are playing, the person who guesses the location first becomes "it."

Comments: After this activity, students really seem to appreciate more the purpose of latitude lines, longitude lines, and directions. Students enjoy this game thoroughly and may spend much time on their own playing it. It makes a good activity after regular work has been completed, and students need something to do.

If played often, students should become very knowledgeable of the locations of places in the world. Students may want to add more places to map on pages 8 and 9 or use another, more detailed map of the world.

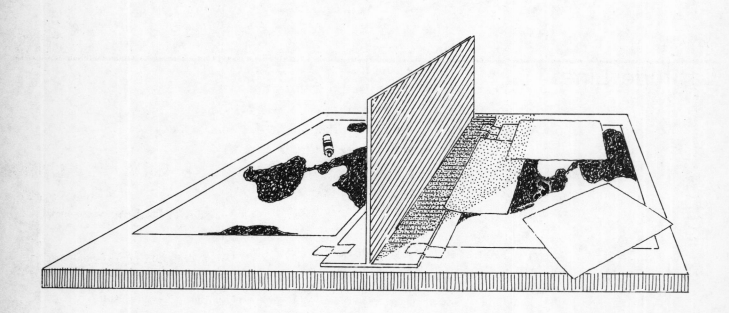

LATITUDE AND LONGITUDE

*To be used as a resource for students to keep in their notes. They may choose to color dotted lines one color and solid lines another, and indicate color by filling in key.

30°W   0°   30°E

NORTH

Longitude Line

PRIME MERIDIAN

England

Longitude Line

20°N   20°N
Latitude Line

↑N ★EQUATOR★   N↑

↓S   S↓

20°S   20°S
Latitude Line

SOUTH

KEY   COLOR

Latitude —— ○

Longitude----- ○

7

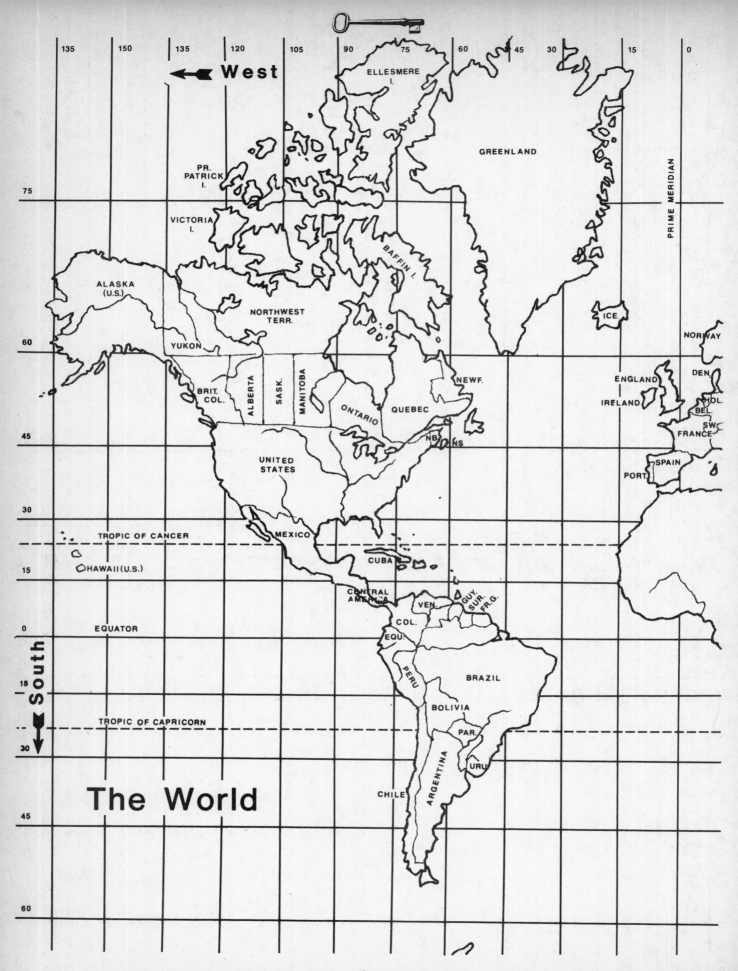

The World

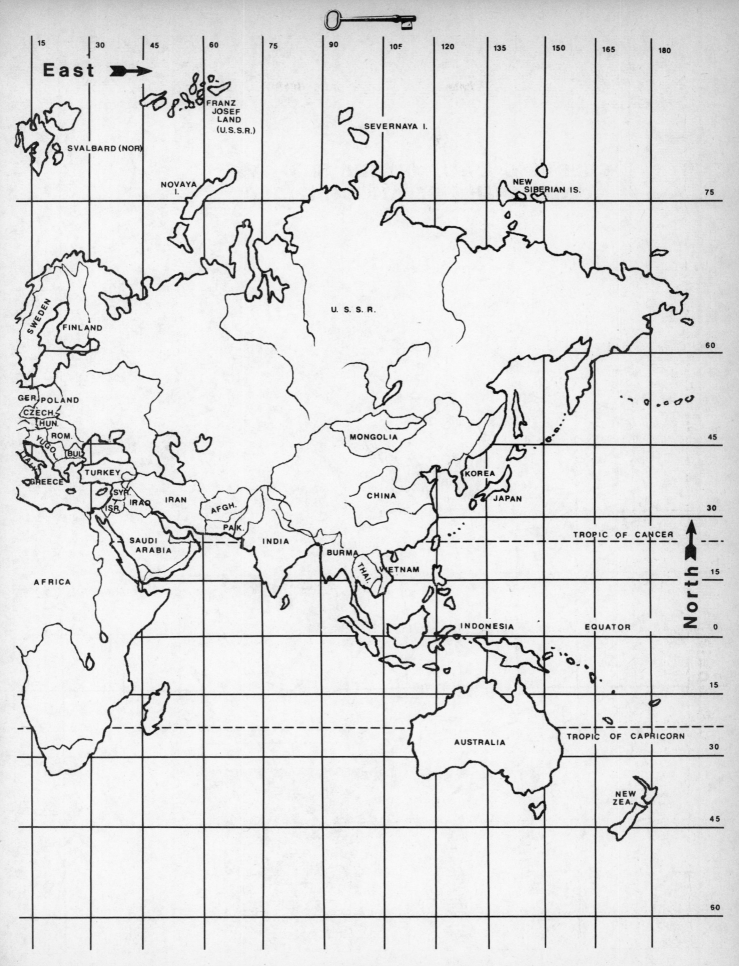

East ➤➤

15 30 45 60 75 90 105 120 135 150 165 180

SVALBARD (NOR)

FRANZ
JOSEF
LAND
(U.S.S.R.)

SEVERNAYA I.

NOVAYA
I.

NEW
SIBERIAN IS.

75

SWEDEN

FINLAND

U. S. S. R.

60

GER. POLAND
CZECH.
HUN.
ROM.
YUGO.
BUL.
GREECE
TURKEY
SYR.
ISR. IRAQ
IRAN
AFGH.
PAK.

MONGOLIA

45

KOREA
JAPAN

CHINA

30

SAUDI
ARABIA

INDIA

BURMA

THAI.
VIETNAM

TROPIC OF CANCER

AFRICA

15

INDONESIA

EQUATOR

North ↑↑

0

15

AUSTRALIA

TROPIC OF CAPRICORN

30

NEW
ZEA.

45

60

9

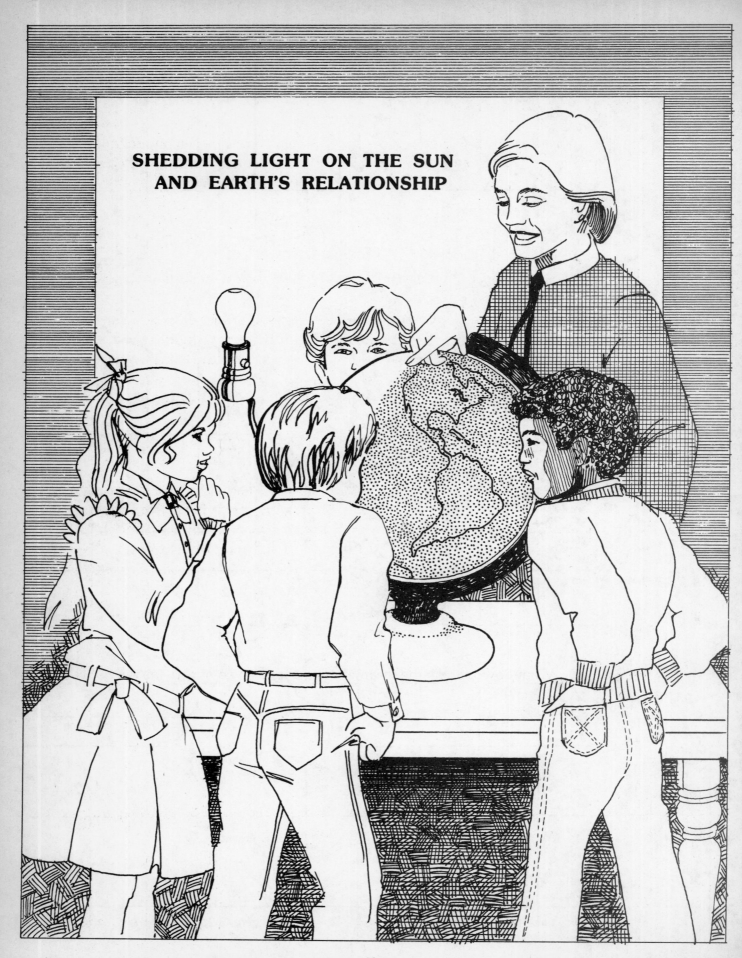

SHEDDING LIGHT ON THE SUN
AND EARTH'S RELATIONSHIP

SHEDDING LIGHT ON THE SUN AND EARTH'S RELATIONSHIP

Activity: A teacher demonstration of the earth's rotation and revolution around the sun and prompted questions lead to further understanding of climatic changes in the world and other global facts (see objectives).

Material:
1. upright lamp with shade removed
2. table
3. globe that is at 23½° on its stand

Objectives:
1. Students will learn the further north or south you are from the equator, the colder it is and why.
2. Students will learn the Northern Hemisphere is warmer in summer and colder in winter and vice versa with the Southern Hemisphere.
3. Students will learn the United States is closer to the sun in the winter than in summer (91,500,000 miles versus 94,500,000 miles).
4. Students will learn earth's tilt creates seasons as it journeys around the sun.
5. Students will learn the relation of latitude, our earth's revolutions, and our seasons.

Directions: Students stand in a large circle around setup. The setup is a lamp (with shade removed) on a table. Room is darkened, and lamp is turned on. Teacher takes globe and slowly turns it around sun and stops at four places to discuss seasons (refer to positions A, B, C, and D on page 13). The teacher leads into concepts (objectives above) by asking questions similar to the following, as he has the globe in the four positions.

Position A: Q. Where are the sun's direct rays?
(winter) R. Southern Hemisphere or Tropic of Capricorn*

Q. What do you think the weather's like above angle of rays (above 30°N latitude)?
R. Cold

Q. Why?
R. It isn't receiving the direct rays of the sun.

Q. What do you think the weather is like in the Southern Hemisphere?
R. Warm

Q. Why?
R. It is receiving most of the direct rays of the sun.

*It should be explained that the areas near and between the Tropic of Capricorn and the Tropic of Cancer are warm year-round, because they always receive much of the direct angle of the sun's rays.

Position A: Q. Did you know we are really closer to the sun in the winter? Why is it still colder in the winter?
               R. The earth's tilt is such that the Northern Hemisphere does not receive as much direct rays from the sun as the Southern Hemisphere.

               Q. What do you think happens in the summer?
               R. Roles are switched.

Position B: Q. Where are the sun's direct rays?
(spring)   R. Equator, equal distribution between North and South Hemispheres.

               Q. Compare weather in Michigan (42°N) and in Argentina (42°S).
               R. Same

Position C: Q. Where are the sun's direct rays?
(summer)   R. Tropic of Cancer, angled upward at Northern Hemisphere

               Q. Which hemisphere is warmest?
               R. Northern

               Q. What makes the Northern Hemisphere warmer?
               R. The earth's tilt is such that the Northern Hemisphere is receiving a more direct angle of the sun's rays.

Position D: Q. What other position is like this?
(fall)   R. Spring

               Q. Why?
               R. Sun's angle is directly at equator.

Comments: Most capable students want to know the why's of things and will retain information longer if they do find out. This is a very necessary lesson for more total understanding of map and globe reading. Students can see what happens with the change of seasons, and figure out many of the why's themselves by prompted questions and observation, rather than someone telling them everything.

EARTH POSITIONS FACING SUN (LAMP)

POSITION A—WINTER

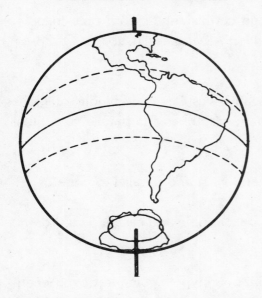

December 22, direct rays are hitting all places along the Tropic of Capricorn.

POSITION B—SPRING

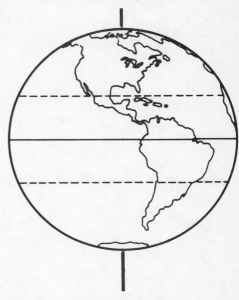

March 21, sun's direct rays are hitting the equator, (days and nights are of equal length everywhere).

POSITION C—SUMMER

June 21, sun's direct rays are hitting all places along the Tropic of Cancer.

POSITION D—FALL

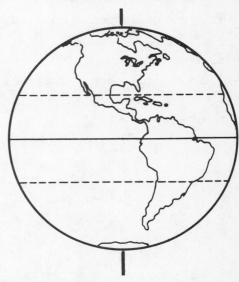

September 23, sun's direct rays are hitting the equator (days and nights are of equal length everywhere).

VOCABULARY

The words below have to do with the earth, and students will need to know them to understand the globe, maps, and the earth's relation to the sun. Teacher may introduce where appropriate. Students may put in their dictionaries.

1. axis: imaginary line, cutting through earth's center from pole to pole; points in the direction of the North Star and tilts at about a 23½° angle.

2. equator: imaginary line running east and west around middle of globe dividing the North and South Hemispheres and parallel to latitude lines. It is 0° latitude.

3. latitude: imaginary lines running east and west and parallel to equator

4. longitude: imaginary lines running from pole to pole and east and west of the prime meridian

5. prime meridian: an imaginary line running from pole to pole going through Greenwich, England. Longitude lines go east and west of this line which is 0°.

6. revolution: earth's path around the sun which takes approximately 365¼ days.

7. Tropic of Cancer: imaginary line 23½° north of and parallel to equator

8. Tropic of Capricorn: imaginary line 13½° south of and parallel to equator

MEASURING DISTANCE ON A MAP

Activity: Students will measure mileage from one place to another using yarn or string, a near accurate way of measuring lines that are not straight, use a scale of miles and apply the skill to AIR AMAZEMENT on page 19 and MEASURING PERIMETERS on pages 20 and 21.

Material: 1. map (distance to measure)
2. page 19, AIR AMAZEMENT
3. pages 20 and 21, MEASURING PERIMETERS
4. string
5. scissors
6. pencil and paper for figuring or a calculator

Objectives: 1. Students will learn a process of measuring from one place to another on a map.
2. Students will learn a process of measuring the perimeter of an area.
3. Students will strive for accuracy in measuring.
4. Students will come up with as many different combination routes between seven different cities in AIR AMAZEMENT as possible.

Directions: A. Measuring from one spot on the earth to another
Step 1:   Take a piece of string and, starting at one end, stretch it from one spot on the map to another (from Xville to Yville).

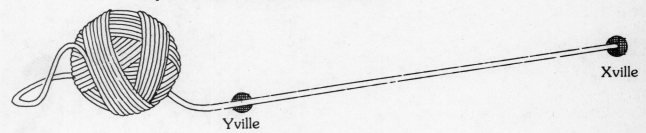

Step 2:   Cut string at point of destination (Yville) so yarn piece is exactly the length between two spots.

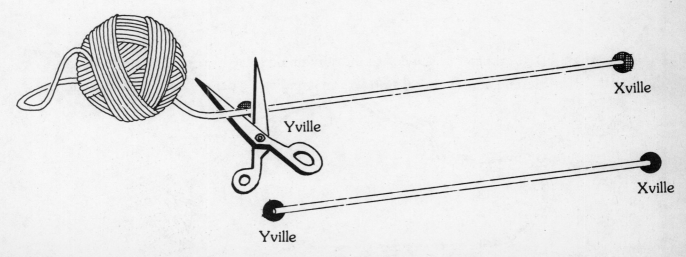

Step 3:   Compare string piece to scale.

1. Hold string piece to scale of miles on map, starting with one end of string and 0 miles.

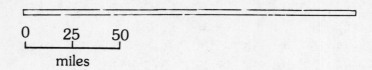

2. Pinch string at end of miles and bring pinched part to 0. Write down miles to pinch.

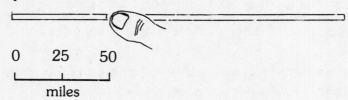

3. Keep doing this until you get to end. Add all parts together to get total mileage.

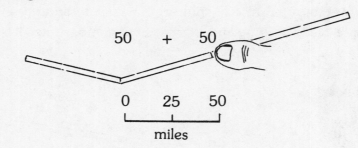

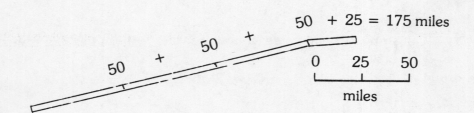

Directions: B. Perimeter: distance around something (May want to insert in dictionary.)

Step 1:   Starting at one end of string, form string along perimeter of area measuring.

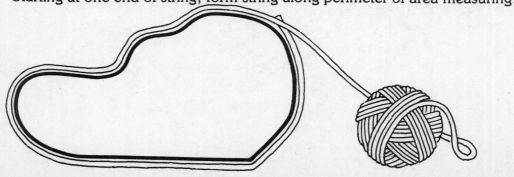

16

Step 2:   Cut string where it meets.

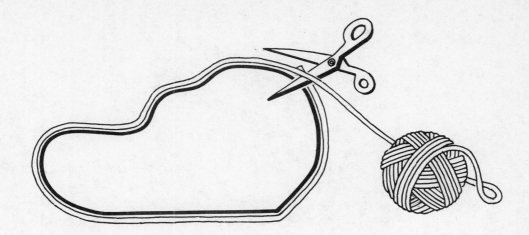

Step 3:   (Optional) If you want measurement more accurate, go over perimeter with string again—only this time mold with your fingers to fit perfectly. Then pinch to hold a place (probably a corner). Then pull out excess string and keep going. You'll probably end up with excess string that needs more cutting.

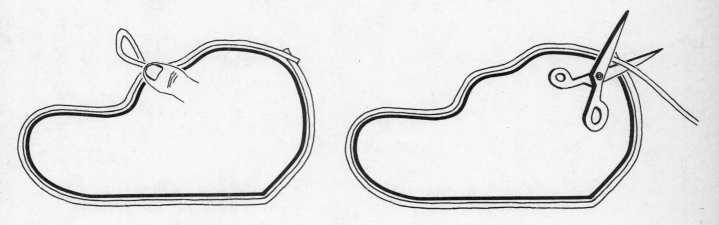

Step 4:   Measure same way as A (Step 3) along scale of miles.

Comments: The accuracy of calculating the number of miles around the perimeter of each state from the maps on pages 20 and 21 will not be exactly correct as the true geographical detail of each state's borders and shorelines cannot be depicted on such maps. Students need to be aware that they can only come up with an approximate figure. The teacher may want to ask the students why this is so. String (especially for the perimeter) makes a measurement possible, because you can contour it to the shape. With maps that show more shoreline detail, a finer piece of string should be used.

Extension: For more opportunities at figuring out perimeter, have students figure the perimeters of the states on pages 119 and 120. They then should be more than ready to try figuring the perimeter of any area on any map.

AIR AMAZEMENT

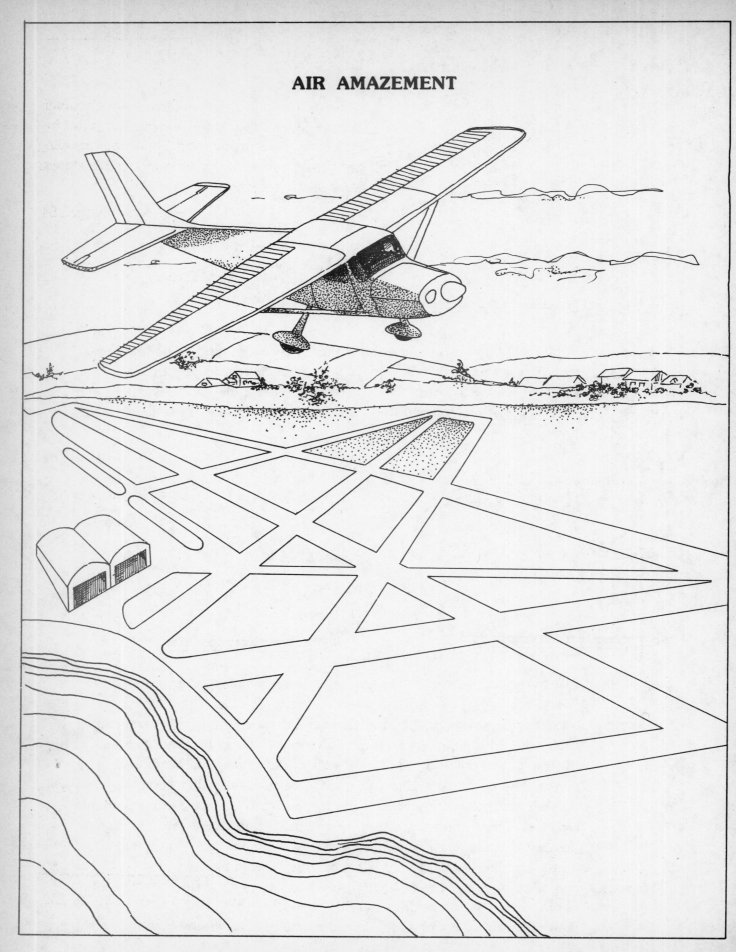

AIR AMAZEMENT

A City
◉

B City
◉

Student Directions: As an airline programmer, your responsibility is to plan all possible flights between the cities below and figure the traveling distances between them. Figure measurements from the middle dots.

Answers on page 151.

C City
◉

E City
◉

G City
◉

D City
◉

F City
◉

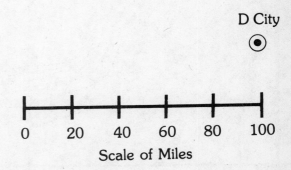

Scale of Miles

MEASURING PERIMETERS

Student Directions: Figure out the perimeters of the areas on pages 20 and 21, using string and your scale of miles.

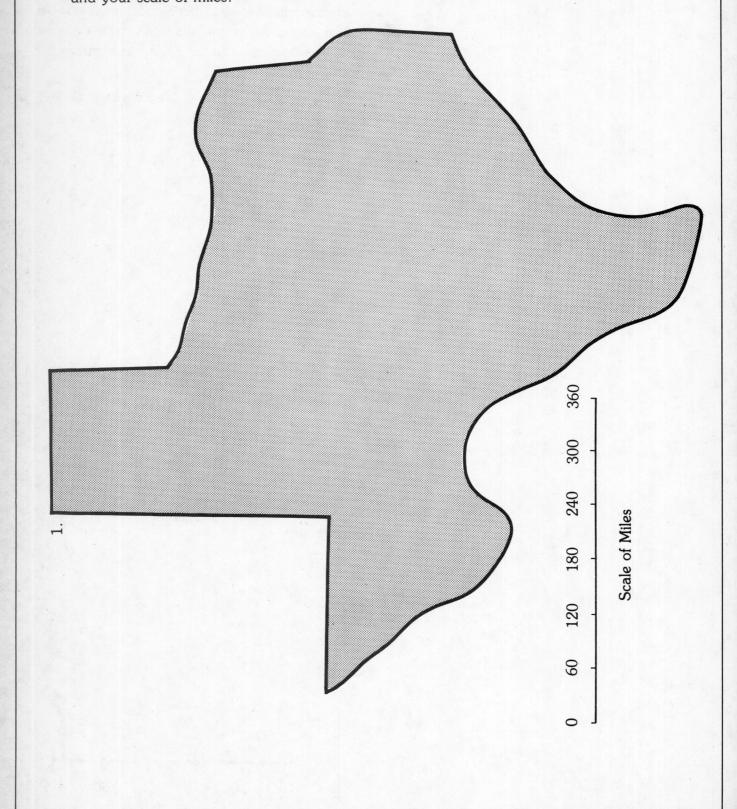

1.

Scale of Miles

0   60   120   180   240   300   360

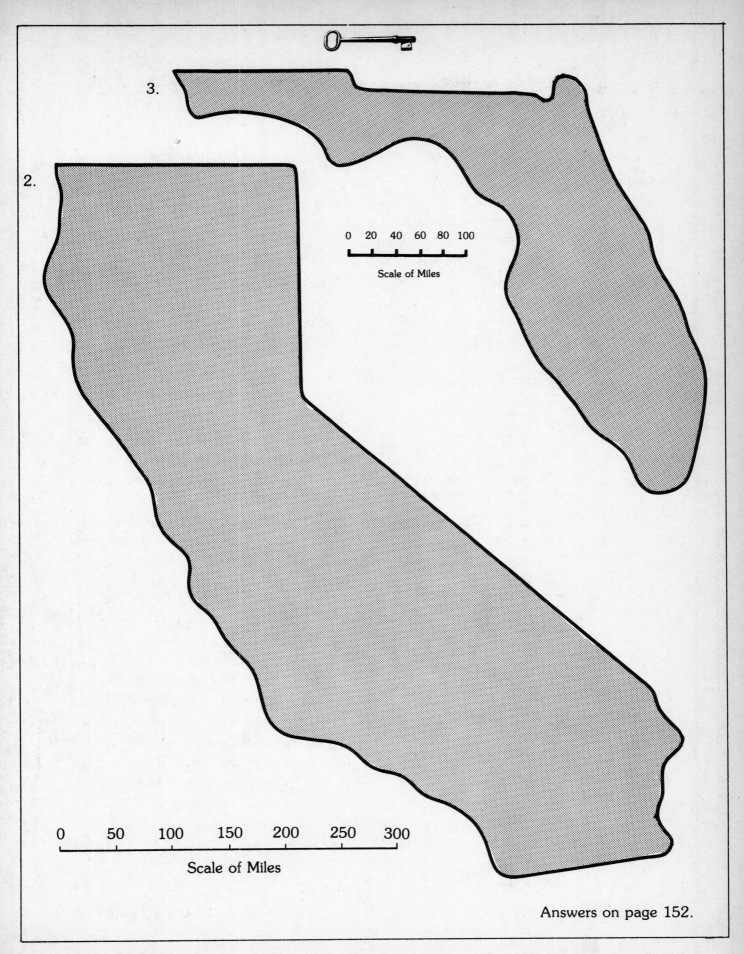

3.

2.

0 20 40 60 80 100

Scale of Miles

0 50 100 150 200 250 300

Scale of Miles

Answers on page 152.

FIGURING THE TIME IN DIFFERENT PARTS OF THE WORLD

Student Directions: Refer to a chart on time zones in an atlas to answer the questions below.

1. What time is it in Los Angeles, California, on your chart?_____
2. What time is it in New York, New York, on your chart?_____
3. How many hours are there between Los Angeles and New York?   (Subtract Los Angeles' time from New York's time.)_____
4. What time would it be in New York if it was 7:00 in Los Angeles? (Add the answer to number 3 to 7:00 because the hours increase as you go east or right on the map.) _____

Using this approach to figure your answers, fill in chart below.

TIME	
Los Angeles	**New York**
1:00	
5:00	
12:00	
10:00	
9:00	

Note: If you add two numbers and get an answer over 12, you have to subtract 12 from your answer to find the time you are looking for. For example, if it was 7:00 someplace (Y) in the world and you wanted to know what time it was 7 hours away east (X), simply add 7 + 7 and get 14. Subtract 12 from 14, and you get 2. It is 2:00 at X when it is 7:00 at Y.

5. What time would it be in Los Angeles if it was 12:00 in New York? (You subtract the answer to number 3 from 12:00 because the hours decrease as you go west or left on the map.) _____

Answers on page 152.

Using this approach to figure your answers, fill in chart below.

TIME	
Los Angeles	New York
	10:00
	12:00
	3:00
	8:00
	1:00

Note: If you subtract a larger number from a smaller number, you get a negative number. Simply subtract the positive of that number from 12 to get the time you are looking for. For example, if it was 5:00 someplace (Y) in the world, and you wanted to know what time it was 7 hours away west (X), simply subtract 7 from 5 and you get −2. 12−2=10. It is 10:00 at X.

6. Fill in the chart below. Make sure you figure out the hour distance between the cities first. Good luck!

TIME			
London	2:00		Madagascar
London	12:00		Madagascar
Alaska		11:00	London
Alaska	11:00		London
Michigan	3:00		Madagascar
Michigan	7:00		Madagascar
Mexico		10:00	Madagascar
Mexico		6:00	Madagascar
Tasmania	4:00		New York
Tasmania		10:00	New York
New York		2:00	London
New York		5:00	London

Answers on page 152.

DO YOU KNOW YOUR ATLAS?

Teacher: Atlases vary somewhat regarding certain kinds of information they may offer. The teacher should make available to students different makes of atlases so if an answer can't be found in one, it should be found in another. A good single atlas to use is *The Signet/Hammond World (pocket) Atlas*, in which all answers can be found.

The questions below may be used as a pretest or a post-test.

Student Directions: Answer the questions below by using your atlas.

1. After looking through your atlas (as we did in class), in your own words describe what an atlas is.

    _____

    _____

2. What types of information do you find in an atlas?

    _____

    _____

    _____

3. What is the highest mountain in the world, and where is it located? _____

    _____

4. What is the name of the longest river in the world, and where is it located? _____

    _____

5. How many miles is it from New York City to Honolulu, Hawaii?_____

6. If it's 2:00 in Michigan, what time is it in England?_____

7. Give the approximate latitudes and longitudes of these places:

    Spain_____   Michigan _____

    Denmark _____   Prague, Czechoslovakia _____

8. Find these places:

   21°N: 157°W:_____   52°S:59W:_____

                    65°N: 20°W:_____

9. How many miles is it from Carson City, Nevada, to Las Vegas, Nevada? _____

10. How many miles is it from Cape Town, Africa, to East London, Africa? _____

11. By studying the map of California, list some characteristics of the state. _____

    _____

    _____

12. What do you think the weather is like in the Falkland Islands around June 21? _____

    Why? _____

13. When would someone need to be accurate with latitude and longitude? _____

    _____

14. What is the distance of Africa's perimeter? _____

15. By studying the maps of Montana and Mississippi make as many comparisons as you

    can find.

    Montana   **Mississippi**

    colder   warmer

16. On a separate piece of paper, devise questions for your classmates to look up.

Answers on page 152.

ATLAS TEAM QUIZ BOWL

ATLAS TEAM QUIZ BOWL

Activity: Two teams of four to six students compete to see how fast they can locate information in the atlas in a quiz bowl.

Material:
1. questions and answers on pages 28 and 29 in this book, or questions and answers students have submitted. (They should be reviewed and accepted by teacher ahead of time.)
2. atlases—either different atlases available to each team or the same make of atlas for all students. If using only one kind of atlas, *The Signet/Hammond World* (pocket) *Atlas* is strongly recommended.
3. sign ATLAS TEAM QUIZ BOWL (optional)

Objectives:
1. Students will interpret information in atlas.
2. Students will learn numerous facts about the world.
3. Students will locate information in an atlas quickly.

Directions: Teams of four to six students each are equally positioned from teacher. The teacher reads questions on the atlas to teams. A member from each team is "it" and the one who can locate the answer first receives a point for his team.

The teacher should assign the job of scorekeeper to someone who is not a team member. The team with the most points at the end of the bowl is the winner.

Note: Students should be familiar with the types of questions that will be asked ahead of time so they can study for the bowl. Either ask questions similar to those on page 28 or have students answer questions on page 28 for preparation. If students submit their own questions and answers for use in the bowl, make sure you don't give someone his own question.

Comments: Students generally will put a lot of effort into preparing for this, because most students love the challenge of competing against fellow classmates. If they think up questions for the quiz bowl, they are even more enthused. However, the teacher should set guidelines for the types of questions ahead of time. For instance, an answer should not take very long to look up or figure out. This is a wonderful activity for reinforcement of everything students have up to now.

ATLAS TEAM QUIZ BOWL QUESTIONS

Teacher: Make sure these questions can all be located in the atlas(es) the teams are using. They can all be found in *The Signet/Hammond World* (pocket)*Atlas.*

1. What is the largest ocean?
2. Whose flag is exactly half red and half white?
3. What is the sea north of Africa?
4. What divides Spain and Morocco?
5. Where is the Sulu Sea? Locate it.
6. What is the name of a country that Lebanon touches?
7. How far is it from Las Vegas, Nevada, to the bottom tip of the state?
8. What is the longest river in the United States?
9. What is the longitude of Mexico City, Mexico?
10. What is the latitude?
11. How many square miles is the Baltic Sea?
12. What country is located at approximately 20°N and 75°W?
13. In what continent are the tallest mountain ranges?
14. What is the population of Michigan?
15. What is the square mileage of Greece?
16. What ocean is between the Americas and Asia and Australia?
17. How many seas surround Europe?
18. What time is it in Michigan when it is 4:00 in Moscow?
19. What is the largest mountain in America?
20. What sea divides Egypt and Saudi Arabia?
21. What is the length of Wyoming?
22. What state is more populated, Texas or Nevada?
23. What is the climate of Michigan?
24. What country is at approximately 30°N and 50° E?
25. What is the population of Egypt?
26. What sea is north of Europe?
27. What country is located at approximately 40°S and 170°E?
28. What is the air distance between Chicago and Tokyo?
29. Whose flag has a leaf on it?
30. What continent is more heavily populated, North America or Asia?
31. Where is Spain?
32. Where is Quebec?
33. How many miles is it between Tokyo and Yong Yang, North Korea?
34. What is the vegetation of the northern part of South America?
35. What is the largest sea in the world?
36. What is the air distance between Chicago and New York?
37. When it is 6:00 in Alaska, what time is it in Michigan?
38. What is the longitude of Tasmania?
39. What is the latitude?
40. What is the greatest depth in feet of the Pacific Ocean?
41. Lake Michigan is the _____ largest inland lake in the world.
42. What land is at approximately 65°N and 20°W?
43. What ocean is between the Americas and Europe and Africa?
44. Where is Switzerland?
45. Where is Burma?
46. What is a name of a heavily populated country?
47. What is the vegetation of Michigan?
48. What ocean is between Africa and Australia?
49. How many miles is it between Sardinia Island and Sicily?
50. What is the perimeter of Sweden?

ATLAS TEAM QUIZ BOWL ANSWERS

Note: Teacher should allow for students' fluctuation in measuring.

1. Pacific
2. Indonesia, Monaco, or Poland
3. Mediterranean
4. Strait of Gibraltar
5. northwest of Malaysia
6. Syria or Israel
7. approximately 80 miles
8. Mississippi
9. approximately 99°W
10. approximately 19°N
11. 163,000
12. Cuba
13. Asia
14. Answers will vary with updating of atlas.
15. around 50,944
16. Pacific
17. 7
18. 9:00
19. McKinley
20. Red Sea
21. approximately 350 miles
22. Texas
23. humid
24. Iran
25. Answers will vary with updating of atlas.
26. Norwegian, Barents, or Greenland
27. New Zealand
28. around 6,313 miles
29. Canada
30. Asia
31. Teacher will verify when student locates it.
32. Teacher will verify when student locates it.
33. approximately 800 miles
34. Tropical Rain Forest
35. Caribbean
36. around 714 miles
37. 11:00
38. approximately between 145°E and 148°E
39. approximately between 43°S and 45°S
40. around 36,198
41. 6th
42. Iceland
43. Atlantic
44. Teacher will verify when student locates it.
45. Teacher will verify when student locates it.
46. Teacher will verify on a map of population.
47. broadleaf forest and/or coniferous forest
48. Indian
49. approximately 160
50. approximately 2700 miles

009'S LOST SECRET AGENT

009'S LOST SECRET AGENTS
(Mind bender)

Activity: Student will solve the mind bender on pages 32 to 33 by using some systematic approach.

Material: 1. "009'S LOST SECRET AGENTS" mind bender on pages 32-33
2. atlases, globes, almanacs, world resources
3. string for figuring mileage
4. paper, pencils
5. matrix on page 34 if teacher feels it is needed to help get students started.

Objectives: 1. Students will locate places on maps.
2. Students will locate and interpret flags.
3. Students will interpret climate by latitude.
4. Students will figure mileage.
5. Students will interpret population maps and tables.
6. Students will interpret time zones.
7. Students will interpret latitude and longitude.
8. Students will locate capitals.
9. Students will interpret size of countries.
10. Students will interpret tables on principal mountains and longest rivers.
11. Students will apply facts from the atlas or globe to solving problems.
12. Students will learn numerous facts from atlases.
13. Students will stick to a task until it is finished.
14. Students will analyze information.
15. Students may become team members, with the responsibility to carry their own weight towards the teams' goals.
16. Students will interpret atlas indexes.

Comments:

This has proven to be a very challenging learning activity that is fun for all! It can be given to individual children, to partners and to teams to work on. Giving it to individual students seems to work the best because the activity's solution requires a sequential pattern of figuring it out, and if many people are involved it becomes lost. However, it has proven successful with teams that are organized and work well together. Sometimes one person misses what another sees. For instance, did you notice that Agent E is a woman? It is one of those activities that demands the team to become organized and work together for success, similar to higher level management teams of successful businesses working towards a solution to a complicated company problem.

A word of caution—not all gifted students may be able to handle this to the end, but all should be able to participate on a team. The activity can be a challenge to those who just want to try it. Usually all want to try it. Then it becomes the discussion of the week. Students help one another and do a lot of comparing of answers.

009'S LOST SECRET AGENTS
(Mind bender)

Student Directions: Read over mind bender "009'S LOST SECRET AGENTS." Then help Secret Agent 009 match the twelve lost agents to the countries in which they belong, by doing research using available atlases, world maps, globes, and/or other resources.

Secret Agent 009 has a big problem. An important computer print-out of twelve other secret agents and their home bases (places where they're currently assigned to live) was stolen—an act of espionage. Secret Agent 009 needs desperately to know where these agents are, so he can help solve an important case. He has some notes he's taken on the agents in the past month that he hopes will give him some clues as to the agents' whereabouts. The agents' names are coded from A to L. The places where they belong are Australia,* Brazil, Canada, Egypt, France, India, Iran, Japan, Mexico, New Zealand, South Africa, and the United States. Using 009's notes below as clues, can you help him match the agents to their correct countries? 009 will not forget your help!

CLUES

1. Agent C took a ship across the ocean from his home base to Spain under a different name.

2. Agent E flew over 8000 miles (shortest distance) from her home base to Madagascar, thinking no one would follow her there.

3. Agent I supports his red and white flag.

4. Agent K will not be able to use his trick, cross-country skis, because of his country's typical lack of snow—even in its colder months.

5. Agent L has asked for a less populated country for his next assignment so he can move about faster. Over 200 people per square miles are too many people for him.

6. Agent A departed from home base on June 21 at 6:00 p.m.—reached destination in Brazil, five hours behind home base.

7. Agent G will be transferred to a submarine from a ship in one of two seas (Arabian or Red)—both less than 3000 miles away from home base.

8. Agent B made contact with three agents on his side of the world, between 130°W and 30°W.

9. Agent D's main responsibility is to watch for infiltration from the sea, because no one can infiltrate by land.

*For simplicity, Australia is included as a country.

10. Agent H is concerned about one of the six countries that it borders.

11. Agent J is requesting to move across the strait, which would still keep him in his country.

12. Agent F was born in one of the largest countries in the world, over 3,000,000 square miles, where he resides now.

13. Agent D has touched base at his country's capital, C...(can't read name of capital other than first letter).

14. Agent K is relocating to capital, located at the beginning of an important delta.

15. Agent B's main responsibility is to keep an eye on the border crossing of one of the world's longest rivers, which divides his own country and the only female agent's country.

16. Agent F will meet his girlfriend, none other than the agent from the country his country borders.

17. Agent H was positioned on purpose NW of Agent G.

18. Agent L was sent to home base in the mountains over 14,000 ft. high, because he has been trained in such mountains.

Answers on pages 153 and 154.

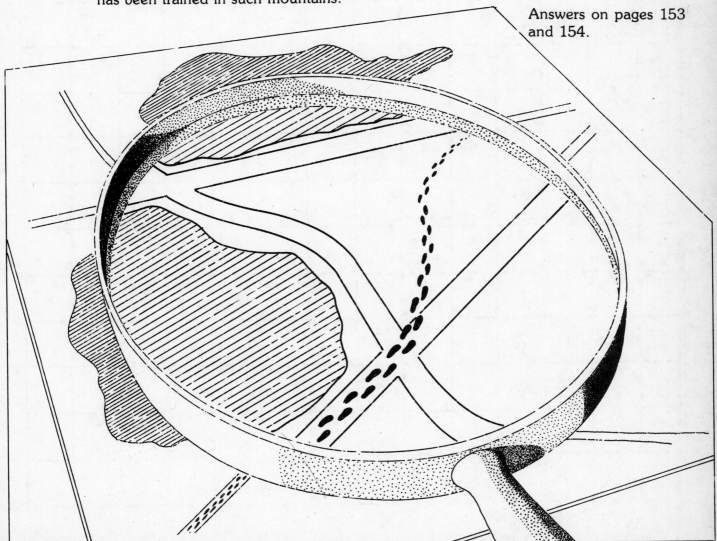

009'S LOST SECRET AGENTS
(Mind bender)

Student Directions: The matrix below is to X out all possible countries the agents could not be in. When you've located an agent, star the square in the column in which his/her country is and X out all squares in the country and letter columns.

	Australia	Brazil	Canada	Egypt	France	India	Iran	Japan	Mexico	New Zealand	S. Africa	United States	Special Notes
A													
B													
C													
D													
E													
F													
G													
H													
I													
J													
K													
L													

Answers on pages 153 and 154.

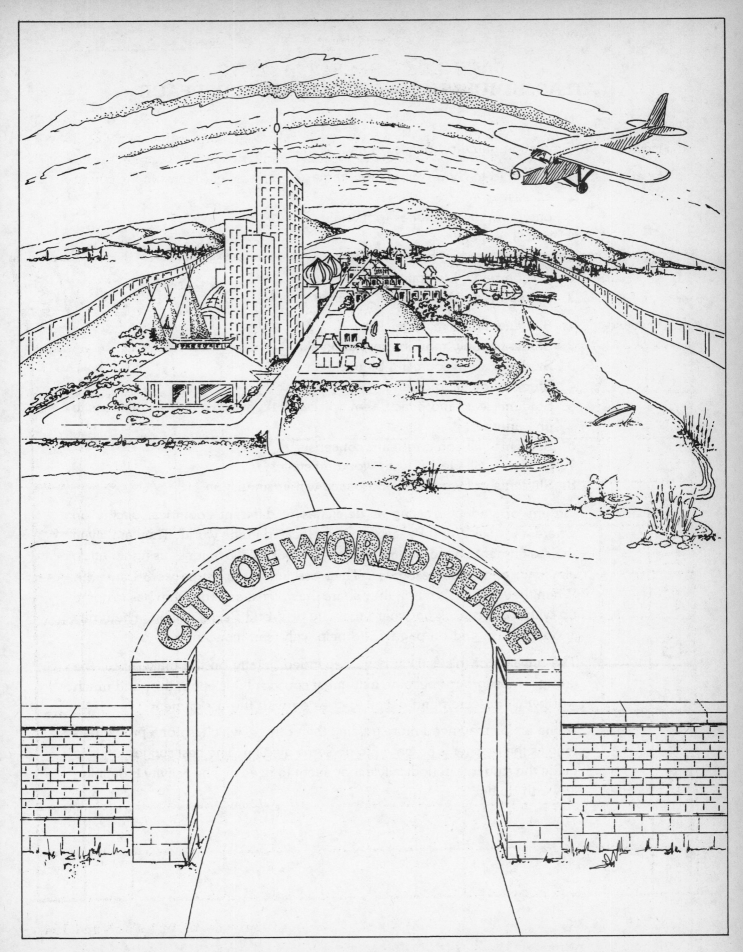

ATLAS SIMULATION — CITY OF WORLD PEACE

Activity: Simulation game on pages 38 and 39.

Material: 1. pages 38 to 39 on simulation game
                2. atlases
                3. other worldly resources (optional)
                4. pencil, paper
                5. string
                6. grid on page 42 (optional)
                7. survey on pages 40 and 41 (optional)

Objectives: 1. Students apply mileage skills.
                2. Students apply map interpretation skills.
                3. Students are resourceful by using atlas.
                4. Students develop criteria.
                5. Students learn more facts about places in the world and their relations to one another.
                6. Students will come to team concensus.
                7. Students will identify with world delegates.
                8. Students will work at world peace within simulation.

Directions: Groups of students, acting as delegates of different countries, decide on where a City of World Peace should be located in the world. They are given the assignment ahead of time to research possible locations, using an atlas, almanac, and other resources. Their assignment is on pages 38 and 39. When they meet as a team, they share their ideas, and the team has to come up with a concensus on where the City of World Peace will be. They may choose to use grid on page 42 to help with team concensus.

Comments: The rewards of this activity have depended greatly on the make-up of the groups. Most groups become extremely conscientious about this, and much worthwhile research and debating goes on with this assignment.

                Some teams may need more guiding than others, which is not a problem as long as the teacher is prepared to do some guiding. The best suggestion is to guide the students periodically if they seem to need it. The activity is definitely worth doing.

Comments: Listed below are some possible criteria (brainstormed by author's students) which students may think of and use for their City of World Peace.
-conducive climate for all major sports
-comfortable climate
-conducive geographic conditions for all major sports
-not already populated
-easily accessible
-not conflicting with any other world attractions
-not conflicting with anything of importance to the area and/or world
-no main disasters
-not dangerous
-no major political problems
-not a hostile area
-near modernization/civilization
-healthy area
-should not have unusual culture around
-should have a fairly universal language near

Extended
Activities:

1. If students become really involved with this, offer them additional follow-up follow-up challenges. Students, as delegates, could be responsible for sending back a summary on the chosen location to their country. The team should brainstorm things to be included: latitude, longitude, air distances from major cities, year-round climate, etc.

2. The delegates did such an outstanding job, additional challenges (responsiblities) could be given them. They could think of a name for the city. They also could design a flag. It should be unique but still fit in with the designs of national flags.

3. An even more in-depth project would be to have students design new layout of the land for the city. This holds unlimited possibilities from creative thinking to drawing maps to designing small scale replicas of the city.

4. If a team has difficulty coming to a concensus with this assignment, the teacher may want to have students assess their difficulties by filling out pages 40 and 41 and then discussing answers in a group. This will help students leave the activity with their feelings sorted out and help them with future activities in which their team has to come to a concensus.

WHERE WILL OUR NEW CITY OF WORLD PEACE BE?

Student Directions: You and other delegates from around the world are to decide where a city of world peace will be located in the world. Read your assignment below for more specific directions.

Dear Delegate:

You are part of a World Peace Delegation assigned the task of finding a place somewhere in the world that will be the permanent location for a city of world peace. The city will be a combination of a world's fair and the Olympics. It should offer every kind of sport sometime during the year, and be open all year to all nations that promote peace. All peaceful nations may acquire land to build their own ethnic shops, restaurants, and motels for tourists to visit. The city will definitely be a tourist city (fun for all), but the main theme will be "peace throughout the world." The land will become neutral land, belonging to no nation.

Your first responsibility is to develop criteria on your location with the other delegates. Here are some possibilities. The chosen area should have conducive climate and geographic conditions for all kinds of sports. It should not already be heavily populated. It should be easily accessible to get to from all parts of the world, especially from major metropolitan cities. It should not conflict with any other world attractions.

Your next responsiblity is to research, alone, maps and other world resources to find a location that you feel best meets the criteria.

When you have found a prime location or two, bring your ideas and good reasons back to the team, as other team members will do. Team members (delegates) will discuss, debate, argue ideas against and for suggested places for the new City of World Peace. It is your delegation's responsibility to choose one location, the best possible for everyone interested in peace and visiting this new area. **You have to** eventually come to a concensus as to the place. It is suggested you narrow the suggested places to a few. In coming to a group concensus, you could vote on a place, but it should pass by a 4/5th's majority. Or you could rate each suggested location by the criteria it meets. A 10 would be the highest rating; a 1 the lowest. The location with the highest total score would be the best choice for our new City of World Peace. Use the grid on page 42 if your team opts to do this.

Remember this is to help promote world peace, so try to keep this theme within your group. You are a highly trusted and honored delegate, and it is trusted that you and your team will find the perfect place for the City of World Peace.

CITY OF WORLD PEACE
(Survey on attitudinal changes)

Student Directions: Answer questions below that apply. May be used in a discussion group later.

1. What was your corporation's (team's) goal?

2. Did your team accomplish its goal?

3. What problems did your team have in accomplishing its goal?

4. How did you solve them, or list all possible ways of solving them.

5. Were you happy with your team's decision? Why or why not?

6. Was it fair? Why or why not?

7. Do you like working as a team or alone better? Why?

8. List good things about working alone.

9. List bad things about working alone.

10. List good things about working as a team.

11. List bad things about working as a team.

12. What emotions did you feel while working as a team? Explain.

13. Do you feel the same about your team members now as before this activity? Explain.

14. What type of person was easy to work with?

15. What type of person was difficult to work with? (no names)

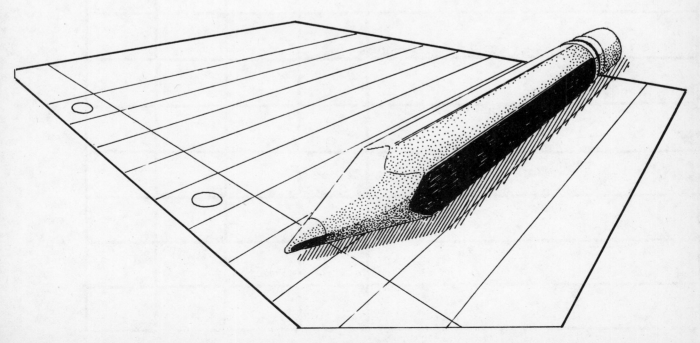

CITY OF WORLD PEACE

(Evaluation grid—optional)

Student Directions: When your team has narrowed its choice for the City of World Peace, fill in grid below with your choice of areas and the criteria you have developed. Then as a team, rate each area 0 through 10 with 10 being the highest score (meeting the criteria 100 percent), 0 not meeting the criteria at all. When you have finished the rating, total scores. The area with highest score will become the City of World Peace.

CRITERIA	AREA			

UNIT II
THE ALMANAC

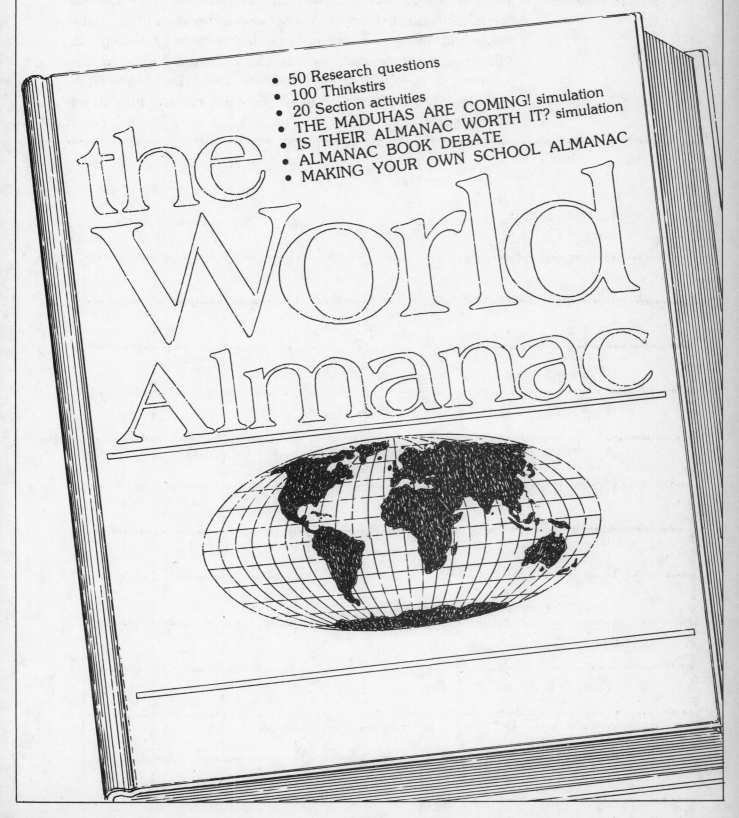

- 50 Research questions
- 100 Thinkstirs
- 20 Section activities
- THE MADUHAS ARE COMING! simulation
- IS THEIR ALMANAC WORTH IT? simulation
- ALMANAC BOOK DEBATE
- MAKING YOUR OWN SCHOOL ALMANAC

the World Almanac

ALMANAC QUESTIONS

Name_____

Student Directions: The almanac is a resource of all kinds of information. That information is only useful to those who know what is there and how to get at it. Look up the answers below in your almanac(s). It is suggested students use one or all of the following current almanacs in their research: *Readers's Digest Almanac; The World Almanac* by NEA; or the *Information Please Almanac*. Researching the questions will give you practice in looking up information in the almanac and, at the same time, familiarize you with what is in it.

1. Who is the governor of Michigan?

2. How much are you worth as a federal tax exemption to your parents?

3. How many calories does a cup of tomato juice have?

4. What is the capacity of the nuclear power plant in Daisy, Tennessee?

5. Who made the first manned space flight?

6. What state produces the most wheat?

7. What college has the biggest enrollment?

8. What is the zip code of Washington, D.C? (District of Columbia)

9. What is the population of Denver, Colorado?

10. What American President received the most popular votes for his election?

11. Who was our tenth President?

12. Who is the army's Joint Chief of Staff?

13. When was Mark Twain (Samuel Clemens) born?

14. Where is the nation of Malawi?

15. When was the Declaration of Independence adopted?

16. What picture won the Academy Award in 1976?

17. How many square miles is the country of Bahrain?

18. What is the nickname of the state you live in?

19. What is the top circulated magazine in the United States?

20. What was memorable about the date 1836?

21. What is the sixth Amendment to the Constitution?

22. Where was Marie Osmond born?

23. What is the last word on the first line of the second verse of "The Star-Spangled Banner"?

24. What is Ringo Starr's original name?

25. Name a country involved with the North Atlantic Treaty Organization?

26. How much is a passport fee?

27. What is the zone called in which most of the world's active volcanoes live?

28. What is the largest island in the world?

29. What rank does Delaware hold in population compared to the other states?

30. What national parks do tourists visit in Texas?

31. What is West Virginia's nickname?

32. Who was the United States women's singles open tennis champion in 1979?

33. When was the first thermometer invented?

34. How far is Jupiter from the sun?

35. How many people died on the *Hindenburg*?

36. What day will your birthday fall on in the year 2000?

37. How many square inches are in a square yard?

38. Who won the football game at the Rose Bowl in 1982?

39. What is the latitude of Nashville, Tennessee?

40. What is the area of the Pacific Ocean?

41. What Heisman (football) trophy winner won two years in a row?

42. Who was the first to explore Florida for a country?

43. Where is the National Aeronautics and Space Administration located?

44. What is the world's wheat production?

45. What is important about June 14?

46. What television program was viewed by the largest audience last year?

47. What is the world's busiest airport?

48. What is the minimum age you may marry in Alabama?

49. Who was the Pope in 1963?

50. Where were the Summer Olympic games held in 1976?

Answers on page 155.

100 THINKSTIRS

Activities: 100 questions that require the researching of separate sections in the almanac, and at the same time, challenge higher levels of thinking.

Material:
1. almanacs
2. 100 questions found on pages 49 to 54 in this book
3. Other needs vary with activity.

Objectives:
1. Students will become aware of what is in the almanac.
2. Students will remember the kinds of information that can be found in an almanac.
3. Students will become aware of events happening in the world and their relationships to those events.
4. Students will learn numerous facts found in the almanac.
5. Students will analyze situations.
6. Students will evaluate their world.
7. Students will take stands on certain issues and support those stands.
8. Students will solve world problems.
9. Students will think of many alternatives for situations.
10. Students will see reasons for using the almanac as a resource.
11. Students will share ideas with others.
12. Students will think beyond the facts.
13. Students will gain confidence from understanding their total world more.
14. Students will be motivated about certain facts to pursue further research to find answers to their questions.

Directions: THINKSTIRS were mainly designed to introduce students to the kinds of information that may be found in the almanac and to arouse interest in it, so they will remember what can be found when needed. Thus, the teacher may guide students where to find the information; then ask the questions to give some purpose to the information that can be found in certain sections.

The teacher may read one (or a group if related) of the 100 provocative questions on pages 49 to 54 to students as a group. Students could see the pages and select for themselves the ones they want to research. However, group discussion on the same topic will create more piggybacking of ideas, which will stimulate better ideas and give students a chance to argue and share in constructive ways.

The teacher may choose which ones he feels the group would enjoy the most. Of course, all of them could be asked over a period of time, which would give a more thorough overview of what is in the almanac.

THINKSTIRS are great fill-ins when you need something to do.

Most of the questions should work well as creative writing assignments and should also stimulate interest in artwork which could be displayed on bulletin boards.

Page numbers of follow-up activity ideas are included where appropriate.

Comments: Students, like most of us, enjoy giving their opinions on issues and become much more involved with the issue if allowed to do so. The teacher acts as a facilitator in most of these cases if done as a group. It's interesting how one or two questions may not spark a great deal of added interest with one group, and then stimulate another into in-depth discussions about it. If the latter happens (it will more often than not), the teacher should guide the students to pursue the issue farther. A panel discussion or debate could be scheduled. Individual research and reports could be assigned. Student products such as a poster or a filmstrip is another alternative.

To summarize, do not cut students' discussion and interest off. The questions on the following pages were designed to create interest and enthusiasm so students would research, think, share, think some more, and acquire a thirst for more.

THINKSTIRS
(100 Provocative questions that will stir you to think!!!)

Student Directions: Teacher will read question or group of related questions below. Research in your almanac, and share your ideas with your class.

1. After looking through your almanac, how are an almanac and an atlas alike?
2. How are they different?
3. How do you think an almanac is like a gifted person?

4. Find the nicknames of the states in the United States. Why do you think they were nicknamed such? Read the summaries of the states in your almanac to see if you were right.
5. After reading the summaries, what new nicknames for some of the states can you come up with?
6. Can you find a unique fact about each state?

7. Based on summaries of some cities in the United States, find one you'd like to visit. Why?
8. Based on summaries of some cities, find one you'd like to move to. Why?
9. Based on summaries, is there a city you would never care to move to or visit? Why?

10. Look up the section on the different countries of the world. What countries haven't you heard of? Can you find something in the summaries of each one that may give you a reason why you haven't heard of it?

11. What countries have you heard of? Why?

12. Using your almanac, how many big differences between the United States and Canada can you come up with?

13. How many big differences between Spain and Switzerland can you come up with?

14. Find two countries you think are very different from one another. How many differences between them can you come up with?

15. Look up countries the United States has given aid to. What countries has the United States given a tremendous amount of money to? What do you think the countries use the money for? (follow-up activity, numbers 4 and 5 on page 56)

16. Can you find some of the largest populated places in the world? What do you think some ill effects for the people of overly-populated areas are? Brainstorm ways to find more room for people.

17. Find the first aid section in your almanac. Which of the emergencies could be avoided in the first place? How?

18. If you were to design a first aid kit to help with these emergencies, what would you put in it? (follow-up activity, number 9, page 57)

19. What words can you think of to describe the tastes of some of the foods listed in the food chart in your almanac?

20. What do you think is the most important food listed? Why?

21. What is the least important food? Why?

22. How many other ways besides eating them, can we use these foods? (follow-up activity, number 6, page 56)

23. If right now you could choose any kind of award listed in the almanac to receive later in life, which one would it be and why?

24. What students in your classroom do you think may be good candidates for some of the awards? Why?

25. Look up the changes concerning income tax from last year. What do you think the best change is and why?

26. What do you think the worst change is and why?

27. Find information about taxes in your almanac. Can you think of many adjectives to describe taxes?

28. Find information on life insurance in your almanac. How do you think life insurance is like a life perserver?

29. Read up on IRA's (Individual Retirement Accounts) in your almanac. Why should someone invest in an IRA?

30. Why shouldn't someone invest in an IRA?

31. If you were ready for retirement, what questions would you have about social security? See if you can find the answers in your almanac.

32. After researching social security in your almanac, do you think we should do away with the social security program? Why or why not?

33. After reading about social security, do you have any concerns about it regarding you some day? What are they? Can you think of some solutions?

34. How does reading the section on social security help you understand older people better?

35. Find some of the world's principal rivers in your almanac. Where are they? How do you think having a large river flow through a country/state affects it?

36. Find some of the world's largest lakes in your almanac. Where are they? How do you think bordering a large lake affects a country/state?

37. How deep do you think the ocean is? Find a table in your almanac on ocean depths. Were you close in your guess? Would you like to travel to the depths of the ocean? Why or why not?

38. What do you think you'd find at the bottom of some of these oceans? (follow-up activity, number 3, page 56)

39. Looking over a list of inventions in your almanac, what do you think was the most important invention of all time?

40. What would life be like without it?

41. Find an invention that was as detrimental as it was beneficial. What was beneficial about it?

42. What was detrimental about it? (follow-up activity, number 11, page 57)

43. Find out through your almanac when women were allowed to vote. What effects did it have in our country?

44. Find a list of the most influencial women last year. Can you think of words to describe these women?

45. If you are a woman, would you want to be on that list? Why or why not?

46. Read information on the office of the presidency in the almanac. Do you think a woman should be President? Why or why not?

47. The motto for the Olympics translated from Latin is "swifter, higher, stronger." Looking up information on the Olympics in your almanac, why do you think the author, Pierre de Coubertin, came up with this? Can you think of other descriptive words that also could stand for the Olympics?

48. Find the section on sports. What do you think is the most difficult sport? Why?

49. Which new sport would you like to try? Why?

50. What sport record would you like to break and why?

51. How would your life change now if you started to train to break the record?

52. What effects would breaking a world's record have on your life? (follow-up activity, number 10, page 57)

53. Find the most popular TV shows of last year. What types of television shows are most popular to Americans?

54. What do you think are some good characteristics of one of the most popular TV shows listed?

55. What show do you think should be included next year? Why?

56. Which show do you think won't be on again? Why?

59. Find a listing of the space flights. Which flight do you think was the most progressive for mankind? Why?

60. Which flight would you like to have been on? Why?

61. Is there a flight you would not have liked to have been on? Why?

62. Do you find all of these flights necessary? Why or why not?

63. What qualities do you think the astronauts of these flights have?

64. Who in your class would make a good astronaut? Why?

65. What are some chief United State's crops? How many ways can you think of that we use some of these crops?

66. Can you think of any unique ways in which we could use these crops?

67. Which crop do you feel you just couldn't get along without? Why?

68. How would life be different for our country if we couldn't produce a major crop?

69. Find something in your almanac that happened 200 years ago that is similar to something happening today. What is it? What are the similarities?

70. Find something in your almanac that happened 100 years ago that is similar to something happening today. What is it? What are the similarities?

71. Find something in your almanac that happened 50 years ago that is similar to something happening today. What is it? What are the similarities?

72. Looking at tables of imports and exports, could the United States be independent of other countries and not go without?

73. Could other countries be independent of the United States and not go without?

74. After reading over the Declaration of Independence in your almanac, if you were the pen that was used to sign the Declaration, how would you feel?

75. What words can you think of to describe the characters that signed the Declaration?

76. Who in your room would most likely have been a signer if they had lived in that time? Why?

77. After reading the Bill of Rights, how would the world be different if the Soviet Union had our Bill of Rights also?

78. Which amendment do you think is the most important? Why?

79. After reading about the Declaration of Independence and the amendments in your almanac, can you think of visible things that stand for our heritage and what this country believes in? (follow-up activity, number 8, page 57)

80. What comparisons can you make between marriage laws in Canada and the United States?

81. Do you agree with the marriage laws of our country? Why or why not?

82. From looking at pages on war, can you think of adjectives to describe war?

83. Find out how much our country is spending on national defense. Should we spend more or less and why?

84. Look up the insignia for different ranks in the services. Can you think of new ideas for the insignia for one of the branches? (insignia not found in *Reader's Digest Almanac*.)

85. Find a calendar in the almanac. Can you think of all the times you need a calendar?

86. Digital calendars are becoming more and more popular. Will they ever do away with the type of calendar in your almanac? Why or why not? (follow-up activity, number 2, page 56)

87. Look over the metric tables. Find units of measures you have used. When have you used them?

88. Can you brainstorm conditions under which someone would need these tables?

89. From reading the section on planets, can you find a unique fact about each planet?
90. What two planets are most alike? How?
91. What two planets are most different? How?
92. Which planet would you most like to visit? Why?

93. After reading about a tornado, a cyclone, a hurricane, (follow-up activity, number 1, page 56) a blizzard, a monsoon, and a flood in your almanac, what types of protection against each one could you take?
94. Is there any place in the world that seems to have a wonderful climate to you, but is very susceptible to these ill effects of climate?
95. Is there any place safe in the world from all of these climatic disasters? Why do you think it is safe?

96. Find a section on zip codes around the United States. What's the difference between the highest zip code and the lowest that you can find? How do you think the post office keeps track of all these numbers?
97. Looking at Postal Information, what things can you think of that the money we pay for postal services is used for?
98. What postal service do you think people use the least? Why?
99. Postal costs keep going up. How do you think we can cut postal costs?

100. If you could meet a famous person (living or dead) listed in your almanac, who would it be? Why? What questions would you ask that person?

20 ACTIVITIES ON DIFFERENT SECTIONS IN THE ALMANAC

Activities: 20 activities that require the researching of separate sections in the almanac.

Material:
1. almanacs
2. activities found on pages 56 to 65
3. Other needs vary with each activity.

Objectives:
1. Students will become aware of what is in an almanac.
2. Students will remember kinds of information that may be found in an almanac.
3. Students will see purpose in using the almanac as a resource.
4. Students will learn numerous facts found in an almanac.
5. Students will have to take facts out of context and present in creative ways.
6. Students will become investigative because of facts found in almanacs and seek information in other resources.
7. Students will analyze situations.
8. Students will identify with different people and different times.
9. Using facts in the almanac, students will create something original to illustrate them.
10. Students will support their opinions.
11. Students will become more familiar with what is happening in today's world.
12. Students will see associations between past and present.
13. Many other objectives will be met by each individual activity.

Directions and Comments: The teacher selects an activity from pages 56 to 65 for students to do and reads it to them. Each activity is self-explanatory. Some activities may be used as follow-ups of the thinkstirs as indicated.

It should be motivating to students if the whole class, or at least a team of students, works on the same activity. However, most of the activities could also be used as individual challenges. Additional comments are given with some individual activities where needed.

1. Using your almanac as a resource for the different kinds of severe weather there are, think up symbols for severe weather warnings. (follow-up of THINKSTIR, number 93, page 54)

2. Look up legal and public holidays in your almanac. Mark on your calendar ones you would like to observe. (follow-up of THINKSTIR, numbers 85, 86, page 53)

3. Make a map of some of the unique geographic features of the world found in your almanac, such as largest seas, deserts, lakes, rivers, and tallest mountains. (follow-up of THINKSTIR, numbers 35-38, page 51)

4. Find the section on country summaries. Locate some of these countries on a map. (follow-up of THINKSTIR, numbers 10-15, page 50)

5. Of the countries above, how many can you find in the newspaper? Why are they in the news? (follow-up of THINKSTIR, numbers 10-15, page 50)

6. Find a calorie chart in your almanac. Using it, plan a day's worth of meals for yourself in which you can not have over 2000 calories. (follow-up of THINKSTIR, numbers 19-22, page 50)

Start keeping track of the calories you consume each day. Write down everything you eat and how many calories every item has for a week. Find the average number of calories you consume in a day. Your total number of calories divided by seven equals your average. Compare it with other members of your class. Locate the average number of calories that should be consumed by you based on your height, weight, size, age, and activity.

7. Look up famous people (politicians, foreign ambassadors, entertainers, etc.) in your almanac. See how many you can find in your city's newspaper. Share with class. You may want to put articles on a school bulletin board.

8. Find the United States' Amendments in your almanac. Find examples of the applications of these amendments in your city's newspaper. How would the stories be different if we had no amendments. Rewrite a story as if we had no amendments. (follow-up of THINKSTIR, numbers 78, 79, page 53)

9. Find the section on first aid in your almanac. With a partner, act out the emergency and the treatment. There should be no talking unless the teacher gives directions to do so. Other students watch and the one who guesses the situation may go next. To save time, all students should have an idea, a partner, and practice time before the actual role playing begins. (follow-up of THINKSTIR, numbers 17, 18, page 50)

10. Research all the sports in your almanac. Combine some characteristics of different sports to come up with a new sport. Develop directions on how to participate and criteria for winning. (follow-up of THINKSTIR, numbers 48-52, page 52)

11. Research all the inventions in your almanac. Design an invention that does what another invention does but in a different way. (follow-up of THINKSTIR, numbers 39-42, page 51)

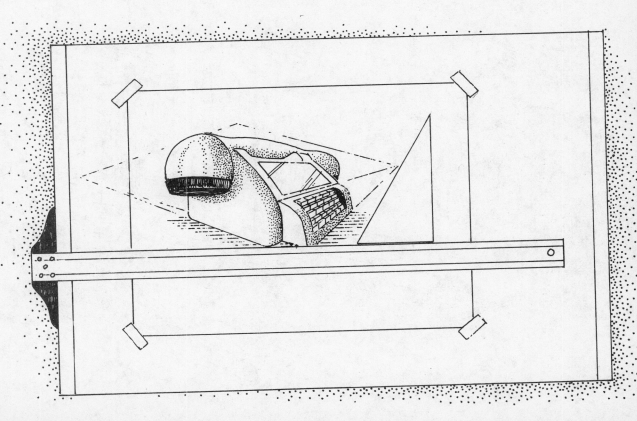

12. Find an association in your almanac you'd like to belong to. Share why with group. Write the association to find out how to become a member. Share correspondence with group.

13. Find top news stories in your almanac. Discuss with your group what they all mean. Which news story do you consider the most important? Why? As a team evaluate the news stories, and out of them select the one your team feels is the most important. You may have to develop criteria on what should determine a top news story and rate each one on the criteria you've developed, ten being the highest score and one the lowest score each news story could receive.

14. Brainstorm all the national news stories since your almanac was published. Which ones merit being top news stories? Check with your almanac each year to see if it agreed with you.

15. Brainstorm why we need to save energy. Brainstorm ways of saving energy. Check your almanac to see if you came up with any ideas it didn't. What ideas did it have that you didn't?

Make a checklist of energy-saving ideas you and your family can do. Have your family check off ones they will do. Bring survey information back to school and make a bar graph of the results. From the results, interpret what areas families are working hardest to conserve. What areas are families neglecting the most?

Design fliers/posters to promote energy conservation.

16. Using the almanac as a resource on United State's history facts, make a time line of what you think are the most important facts. Share with your class, and tell why you feel the dates you selected are important.

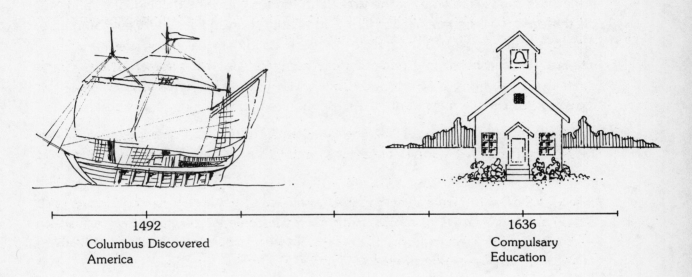

1492
Columbus Discovered
America

1636
Compulsary
Education

17. Brainstorm some effects that would have resulted if some history facts in your almanac had never existed. This may also be done as a creative writing assignment. The teacher may want to put up on a classroom bulletin board.

Examples: What if . . . .

-Columbus had never arrived in America?
-compulsary education had never been established?
-Benjamin Franklin had not been born?
-our constitution was never adopted?
-the Erie Canal had never been opened?
-slaves had never been freed?
-gold was not discovered?
-the Social Security Act had not passed?
-Alaska and Hawaii had not become states?
-the United States had not sent advisers and aids to South Vietnam?
-the United States had not landed on the moon?
-Nixon had not resigned?
-Kennedy had not been assassinated?

18. Pretend the job of President is open to students, and research what the job involves. Students should be able to pick up many facts from most any of the information involving Presidents in the almanac and other resources. The class should form a committee that will set up criteria for being a good President and interview candidates. Either the same committee or another can design advertisements or the office of the presidency. Students can apply for the job and be interviewed by the committee.

If the class chooses to vote for the President, the teacher should decide if it can handle this part. It will be much fairer (not a popularity contest) if an interview committee develops some type of rating scale for each candidate based on the way each answers the questions.

Extension: Students may want to discuss the pros and cons of being President.

19. After finding facts on a President of the student's choice in the almanac, the student becomes the President by doing a biographical sketch of that President. It is important that the student does not tell the facts but acts them out in creative ways in which the audience finds them out only through the acting and talking. Student may also choose to research other information from the time of the President, such as historical facts, inventions, and dress, and try to bring them into the play.

The play should be written first for the teacher's review and editing. If the teacher would put on a biographical sketch first, the students would understand much more clearly what is expected. A sample sketch on John F. Kennedy is available on pages 62 and 63.

Objectives: 1. Students will learn about different Presidents and facts that happened during their lifetimes.
2. Students will have to take facts out of context and put in their own words.
3. Students will identify with other persons.
4. Students will identify with different periods of history.
5. Students will use the almanacs for finding information on Presidents.

Comments: So many students are used to going to a resource (usually the encyclopedia) for information when doing a report and writing down information in sentence form similar to what will be in their reports (not very much of a challenge to their creativity). The type of activity above will not allow for this, because students have to take facts gathered out of context totally and put them into action. This is a really creative and challenging activity for students and one they will enjoy.

BIOGRAPHICAL SKETCH OF JOHN F. KENNEDY
(Activity 19)

*Should be able to find at least fifteen facts about Kennedy in this biographical sketch.

(Kennedy is finishing breakfast with family.) "Good breakfast, Jacqueline. I'm sure glad I married you. You understand all my presidential duties, and you know being the youngest President isn't easy." (Picks up paper.) "Here's a picture of Dr. Martin Luther King in a civil rights peace demonstration. I sure wish him and his movement luck. Well, I've got to go. John, John, finish your milk, and Carolyn be a good girl for Mommy."

Next scene — sign that reads "Oval Office" (Kennedy is looking at his schedule for the day.) "What a busy day ahead of me." (He looks up.) "Oh, a crooked frame." (Goes to straighten frame.) "Am I proud of this, my Pulitzer Prize for *Profiles in Courage*." (Goes back to looking at schedule.) "I sure hope I hear from the premier from the Soviet Union soon about their offensive missiles in Cuba. We don't need a World War III."

(Telephone rings, and he picks up phone.) "Hello. Yes, Mr. Khrushchev. I'm very pleased to hear that. Our country will be relieved to hear you're pulling your missiles out of Cuba. Thank you. Good-by." (Kennedy hangs up phone.) (Calls out door.) "Mr. Press Secretary, set up a press conference as soon as possible."

"Now, where was I?" (Picks up schedule again and sits in his rocker.) "Thank heavens for my rocker. It helps my back that I injured when our PT boat was bombed in the war. Well, at least, I'm lucky to be alive since I was given up for lost."

(The President looks up.) "Yes, Mr. Secretary, press conference in one hour. OK, and I'll have to do some rescheduling with my other plans. Ask Alan B. Shepard if we can meet an hour later. I'm very interested in his trip in space, since I've been trying to accelerate our space programs."

(Phone rings.) "Excuse me." (Answers it.) "Hello. You're concerned about an assassination attempt in Dallas next month because of the large crowds. Yes, you want to keep your 35th President alive. Thank you for your concern." (Kennedy hangs up phone and sits back in chair quietly.) "I wonder if I should be concerned?"

Another way of presenting, in which more action would be demonstrated, is to act out different important years in the life of the President. For instance, the year 1940 when Kennedy injured his back from the bombing of the PT boat he was on and towed a man through the water to the safety of an island could be acted out. Prior to each important year acted out, student should display a card with appropriate year written on it.

20. Student or teacher will select a date out of our history and student will write about it as if he lived during that time ("A Day in My Life in the Year . . ."). Student should research the almanac to find out what was going on (or not going on) during that time in history. The student should bring up as many facts about that time in history as possible but only as part of his writing. He should take note what things had been invented by that time and what things hadn't been. Some other things students could investigate: What laws have been passed by this time? What haven't? What people were influencing the world at this time? Who was President? and on and on. A writing example is on page 65.

Objectives: 1. Students will identify with another time and place.
2. Students will research and learn facts pertinent to time.
3. Students will be creative in weaving facts into a story about a day in one's life.
4. Students will be resourceful by finding information in many different areas of the almanac.
5. Students will become much more familiar with the almanac and see reasons for using it.

Comments: Students don't memorize dates in this activity for the purpose of knowing them. They relate to the time and can see more clearly the relation of historical facts with other facts and times, especially their own.

The more research the student does, the more involved he should become with the time. Hopefully, by the time of this assignment the student will see many areas in the almanac he can use in his research.

If the student becomes really enthusiastic about the time, he should begin asking all kinds of questions such as ... "I wonder if they had a washer and dryer? Could they watch television? What did they do in their spare time? How did they get their news?" ...which should lead into more investigative research into other resources. For example, if one wanted to know what book an eleven-year-old might read during the year 1904, the copyrights of appropriate books could be checked.

A DAY IN MY LIFE IN THE YEAR 1904
(Activity 20)

June 10, 1904

Dear Diary,

I sure had trouble riding Bessy into town today. She hates all those new moving contraptions they call automobiles. Dad says we're going to get one next year. I hate to replace old Bess, but she won't mind being put out to pasture at her age—and she'll love being away from those automobiles.

It sounds like pretty soon we'll be seeing flying contraptions overhead. Well, Dad may be able to get me into an automobile, but not a flying thing. No way!

Well, I have to go, because I have a busy day tomorrow—have to help Mom with the wash, and that's an all day affair. I wish someone would invent something to speed up washing clothes and drying them on a line.

I guess I'll read a little of *Tom Sawyer* before I go to sleep. I'll talk to you tomorrow night.

THE MADUHAS ARE COMING!

THE MADUHAS ARE COMING!

Activity: simulation on pages 68 and 69

Material: 1. almanac (same kind for each student)
              2. simulation on pages 68 and 69

Objectives: 1. Students will become familiar with the almanac.
              2. Students will come to a team concensus.
              3. Students will evaluate what is needed on earth to "fit in."
              4. Students will find things in the almanac that help them cope with society.

Directions: Students read the simulation on pages 68 to 69. Then teams of three to four students decide what ten pages from the almanac would be of the most value to the Maduha family from outer space. They are given the assignment ahead of time. When they meet as a team, they are to share their ideas, and their team has to come up with a concensus on the ten best pages.

Comments: Students may become very serious about finding the best pages in the almanac that will help the Maduhas. This activity really challenges, because students have to analyze their culture, their way of living as human beings (things that are often taken for granted), and decipher what is of most value for survival on earth. Arguing and debating for the pages the students feel are important help the students think about their own value systems.

Student
Directions: Read over simulation, "THE MADUHAS ARE COMING!" Do research in
an almanac on your own. Be prepared with your ten choices and reasons for
them. Each student shares his ideas with team members. The objective of
each team is to come up with a final list of ten pages—meeting with group
concensus.

THE MADUHAS ARE COMING!

The government has hired your corporation (team) to smuggle into the United States
some aliens from another planet in outer space. The Maduha family from Grahusha
(mother, father, daughter, son) look like human beings. However, their ways of living are
totally different from people on earth.

Our government will give these people a home in Michigan and an allotted sum of
money if they will come to our country for a year. We hope they will stay without the public
finding out they are aliens from outer space. It is up to your corporation to come up with information about life on earth to send to the Maduha family, so they can prepare themselves
for life here.

We can send a lightweight envelope through space to them with information. The
envelope can hold ten pages from the World Almanac. It is your responsibility to choose
the ten pages that you feel will help them the most. Remember these people have no idea
what life is like here, and they need to act like they fit in—from eating the way we do to
knowing information about rules in our land.

Here are some examples of what the Maduhas may be like without your help.

1.   Mrs. Maduha puts a vacuum hose up to her mouth thinking it contains food.

2.   Mr. Maduha runs after a car on the highway thinking it's a pet.

3.   A neighbor asks the daughter for a date. He says he'll pick her up on Washington's Birthday. She says "Who's Washington?" He says, "Never mind. Forget our date."

4.   Mr. Maduha digs up his neighbor's lamppost, because he wants to use it as part of a transmitter for communication home.

I mean really! What would the neighbors say? Help the Maduhas out now before these things happen. Don't expect to solve all their problems. They are very quick learners, and will pick things up quickly when they come to earth. But please—get them off on the right foot!

IS THEIR ALMANAC WORTH IT?

(An almanac simulation)

Activity: Two teams, acting as purchasing agents for a major book company, debate if they should purchase 25,000 almanacs or not. They are given the assignment ahead of time so they can research the almanac for preparation.

Material: 1. simulation activity found on page 72 in this book
2. an almanac

Objectives: 1. Students will learn what is in the almanac.
2. Students will analyze parts of the almanac that meet needs of people.
3. Students will see many points of view.
4. Students will see the value of the almanac.
5. Students will debate, discuss, argue in constructive ways.

Comments: At first the almanac (close to 1000 pages) is overwhelming to some students. This is a fun way to get them familiarized with it in a hurry. Also, after this activity, they see the value in the almanac, and this gives credence to learning about it.

Alternative: If the above activity seems too challenging, have all students become the sales representatives for the almanac. The teacher acts as the book company representative. It is the students' challenge to convince the teacher to buy 25,000 copies. State in advance that you, the teacher, will not buy their 25,000 copies unless they can give you thirty or more reasons to purchase it. This activity is extremely fun for students and teacher alike.

Alternative: Students, again, act as sales representatives for the almanac. Only this time, they give individual speeches supporting the almanac. They are doing this to try to get a job as a sales representative for a company, which asked them to do this. The student who writes and presents the best speech will be hired. *

*Teacher may choose to hire all students.

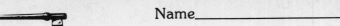

IS THEIR ALMANAC WORTH IT?

You are all purchasing agents for a large nationally known book company. You have just received a purchase order for 25,000 almanacs from a publishing company. One team (half of you) wants to go with the order. We'll call you pro-agents. The other half of you is against the order. We'll call you con-agents. (Teacher will help you decide which team you're on.)

The pro-agents' job is to convince the con-agents the book will sell. The best way to do this is to research the almanac and come up with as many reasons as possible why someone would want to buy the book. For instance, someone who's concerned about dieting and nutrition would appreciate the calorie tables. For every reason you give, your team will get a point. Another point—you wouldn't have to buy an atlas, because the almanac has maps in it.

The con-team's responsibility is to also research the almanac, and find reasons why people would not buy it. "Who wants a chronological summary of last year's hottest news items, when they have already been saturated with this on television and in the paper last year? Another point—if people bought the almanac, then they wouldn't purchase our atlases. Con-agents will get points for thinking of reasons why the book would not sell to 25,000 people. To do this, the team has to research what's in the almanac, and be prepared for the other team to give purpose to the different topic areas found in the almanac.

Each team should take turns with their points and their rebuttals. The team with the most points at the end wins.

ALMANAC BOOK DEBATE

Activity: Two teams of students debate which of two world almanacs, from different publishing companies that the teacher selects, are the best.

Material:
1. almanacs
2. pages 75 to 79 (student directions)

Objectives:
1. Students will debate the quality something has or doesn't have.
2. Students will become aware of what is in almanacs.
3. Students will compare the quality of similar products.
4. Students will learn facts in an almanac.
5. Students will learn to question the value of things.
6. Students will have experience debating.
7. Students will learn that there is more than one way of looking at things.
8. Students will research a product thoroughly.

Directions: See student directions on pages 75 to 79. The teacher should decide what team each student is on. However, if student owns one particular kind of almanac, that should determine his team.

Comments: Students need to thoroughly understand what is expected of them with this activity. They also need to spend a great deal of time on their research. Have students turn in pages 78 and 79 once they've filled them in with research, so the teacher can review them. This will also assure students will put in adequate preparation time for the debate. If the above two points are carried out—that of understanding and research— the debate will be a very valuable experience.

If students have not debated prior to this, their first experience may go a little slow, but once they get into it, they should become very active participators. The rules on page 76 help keep all tempers in place. The debate should become a very constructive form of arguing.

At the end of the debate, students will know their almanacs well. Some may want to purchase their opponent's almanac in place of their own.

Note: The first time a group does this debate, tape it so you can play part of it for another group, who in the future will prepare for the same debate. Listening to the tape will help clarify for students exactly what is expected of them.

Student
Directions: You will be debating which of two similar almanacs is the best. The teacher will inform you as to which team you are on. Once you know which almanac you will be supporting, research both almanacs to (1)find out what types of information can be found in your almanac and not in your opponent's. Every time your team states something your almanac has that the other one doesn't will be a point for your team. (2)Find out what is not offered in your almanac that is in your opponent's, so you can prepare a rebuttal. Two good ways to defend something your almanac does not have are:

1. Give a reason why it is useless or unimportant information.

2. Tell something your almanac has that the other does not.

Use the format on pages 78 and 79 when doing your research.

Refer to pages 76 and 77 for an example of how your debate should run, the giving of points, and the rules. Your team may want to divide up the almanac, and each individual be responsible for a part: pages 1-250 for example or certain categories such as sports and history.

The teacher should keep track of points. There also should be a group of student judges with almanacs in their hands, ready to research information that needs verifying what a team says is true.

ALMANAC BOOK DEBATE

Rules for making points and losing them during the debate:
(Refer to page 77 for interpretation and examples of these rules.)

1. Each team takes a turn making points by stating something that is in their almanac that is not in the other almanac (numbers 1, 2, 4, 6, 9, 11). Individual team members should also take turns unless the one whose turn it is can't think of an example. Then any team member may give an example. If a team divided up the book when doing its research, then the member who is responsible speaks.

2. If a team says the other team's almanac does not have certain information in it and it does and the other team says it does (numbers 2 and 3), then the team that made the statement (Y) loses a point and the team that defended its almanac (X) gets an additional point. A team of judges should verify that the book does have the information in it.

3. A team does not have to make a rebuttal, but if they do they get an additional point. This does not take away from their turn (see numbers 3, 5, 7, 8, and 10).

4. Another tricky way of making a point is to ask the other team why the kind of information in their book (they just mentioned) is important. If they can't come up with why, they lose their point. If they come up with why, the team who questioned loses an additional point (see numbers 6, 7, and 8).

ALMANAC BOOK DEBATE

An example of the way students' debate should go:
(Refer to page 76 for explanation of points.)

1. Team X: "Your almanac has no flags; ours does." (point, no rebuttal)

2. Team Y: "Your almanac doesn't list the states' mayors." (point)

3. Team X: (rebuttal) "Yes, it does." (point, and team Y loses theirs)

4. Team X: "Our almanac has maps in it, and Y does not." (point)

5. Team Y: (rebuttal) "They aren't needed, because most people own atlases." (point)

6. Team Y: "Our almanac has a crossword puzzle guide. Your's doesn't." (point)

7. Team X: (rebuttal) "We don't see any importance in that." (Team X will only get a point if Team Y doesn't come up with something to support why the category mentioned should be in the almanac. Team X is challenging, Team Y with this, and taking a chance at the same time, because if Team Y comes up with support, Team X loses a point.)

8. Team Y: "A lot of people do crossword puzzles indicated by the one in the newspaper every night. Our guide would help all the people challenged by the puzzle and increase their knowledge." (Team Y keeps their point, and Team X loses a point.)

9. Team X: "Our almanac has a chart on food additives that aren't good for you; your's doesn't. (point)

10. Team Y: (rebuttal) "No, but we have a lot of information on the risks of too much sodium intake." (point)

11. Team Y: "Your almanac doesn't tell about the climates of the states." (point)

Total points so far: Team X   Team Y
                                    1 point   4 points

ALMANAC BOOK DEBATE—COMPARING ALMANACS

Name of your almanac (Y) _____

Name of opponent's almanac (X) _____

Student Directions: List types of information found in each almanac.

(Y)	page #	(X)	page #

Information found in Y's but not in X's.	page #	Information found in X's but not in Y's. May want to leave space to write why it isn't necessary, or what yours has instead.	page #

MAKING YOUR OWN SCHOOL ALMANAC

interviewing

topics

who will do what...

History of school   School Bill of rights

The city behind (our) the school

editing

The City behind our School

typewritten

APRIL HILL ELEMENTARY

SCHOOL ALMANAC

finished almanac

MAKING YOUR OWN SCHOOL ALMANAC

Activity: Class will write school almanac, based on *The World Almanac*.

Material:
1. world almanacs
2. paper
3. typewriter (not mandatory)
4. Other needs are based on individual products.

Objectives:
1. Students will be resourceful in finding information about their school.
2. Students will simulate the format of an almanac.
3. Students will plan a project from beginning to end.
4. Students will carry out their responsibilities for a group project if it is to be a success.
5. Students will get to know other students in school better.
6. Students will learn very simple form of an art layout.

Directions:

Step 1:   After reading through world almanac(s), class brainstorms types of information found that could be applicable in a school almanac if you improvised where appropriate.

> Examples:
> 1. Governors of states could be changed to teachers of classrooms or student representatives.
> 2. Top news stories in the world could be changed to top news stories in the school.
> 3. Mean salaries could be improvised to mean grades.
> For more examples refer to page 87.

Step 2:   Class adds new categories for school almanac that aren't in *The World Almanac* but would still be appropriate to a school and its readers.

Step 3:   From brainstormed list, class chooses the categories it wants for its school almanac. Class members select categories that they want to be individually responsible for.

Step 4:   Students fill out sheet on page 84 on how they are going to come up with facts for their particular categories.

Step 5:   Students carry out planning sheet on page 84.

Step 6:   Students write out their reports the way they want them in the book. They proofread, hand into teacher for editing, and then recopy it neatly.

Step 7:   Artwork optional, though it makes a much more interesting book if included and gives students another medium to express their creativity. (See page 86 for directions on art layout.)

Step 8:   Students' final pages need to be typed and Xeroxed if each member of the class is to receive a copy. Parent volunteers should be happy to type such a worthwhile project.

Students should hand into typists neatly written, teacher-edited copies for typing along with art layout, if there is to be artwork.

Step 9:   Students may choose to do other challenges for the book such as:

1. designing cover
2. directory on students who put book together
3. putting together information about the authors of the book (may need to interview)
4. designing a crossword puzzle about classmates or about information in almanac
5. helping other students with research for their project
6. any challenges students come up with that would be appropriate to the book

Step 10:   Given all the copies of the pages of individual student's work, students put together the school almanac the way they want to, but with some order. They should all make a table of contents.

Students should come up with their own way of holding the book together. The teacher should provide all kinds of materials (wallpaper, material, cardboard, rulers, glue, yarn, paper punch, sewing machine). Again, this may be a good place for parent volunteers to assist.

Comments: This is a type of activity you just don't know exactly where it's going to go. But there's one thing for sure, and that is it really appeals to students. They get a chance to write about themselves, their school, and it is for them, and as a result much learning should take place.

Because it involves the school, the teacher ahead of time, should check with the principal, administration and other teachers to make sure they will not mind if their students need help from them and other students with the research process. If you approach them first, you may be pleasantly surprised to get additional help and suggestions that will be a benefit to your whole project.

To carry out this project to a satisfying end, you need to follow through the steps carefully. The carrying out of the individual projects may be somewhat time consuming, and much time needs to be set aside for the project. The students should be given as much time as they want if the interest, caring, and enthusiasm is there, and it should be if the teacher is interested, cares, and is enthusiastic.

The teacher also has to be extremely flexible in allowing students to work on their project when it is convenient to other people in the system who are helping. Also, be prepared—some students will take half as long as others with their projects. The teacher can handle this with his own time management planning.

Students need in-depth projects that demand a lot of planning and steps that lead to an end product, because they need to experience the real business world. When you're in a successful career, you don't do fifteen-minute activities with no long term purpose in mind. You see a long term goal for your company, your responsibility (goal) to help with meeting that goal, steps that lead to your goal, and the way you're going to carry those steps out. Then you implement those steps always with that goal (purpose) in mind. When you reach that goal there is a tremendous gratification with a project well-done and a feeling of success, and success leads to more success. The only way students are going to meet success in that future world is to experience it now and see the worth of sticking to a project.

The school almanac is an extremely worthwhile project which exemplifies all these things and is worth the effort on the teacher's part. The end result will be a lasting treasure to be shared and enjoyed by all for a long time.

SCHOOL ALMANAC PLANNING SHEET

1.   What is your project about?

2.   What questions do you need to have answered?

3.   What are your criteria for kinds of information you need?

4.   What resources will help you find the answers to #2? (If survey is involved, hand in to teacher with this sheet.)

5.   What are you going to do with the results?

SCHOOL ALMANAC PLANNING SHEET
(Example)

1. What is your project about?   School sports records

2. What questions do you need to have answered?

   1. Who is the fastest runner in school? – in each grade?
   2. Who can hit a baseball the farthest?
   3. Who is the fastest swimmer?
   4. Who has caught the largest fish?
   5. Who has been in gymnastics the longest?
   6. Who has the highest bowling average?

3. What are your criteria for kinds of information you need?

   1. Record has to be proved.
   2. Can be in any category of sports.
   3. Should have enough type categories so no group of students will feel left out.

4. What resources will help you find the answers to #2? (If survey is involved, hand in to teacher with this sheet.)

   1. coaches – interview   4. Survey also included.
   2. phys. ed. teacher – interview
   3. students themselves – I'll make a poster informing students what I'm doing and if they think they qualify to bring in proof.

5. What are you going to do with results?

   I'm going to list students' names alphabetically under "record holders," and after each name, write down what record he holds.

SCHOOL ALMANAC—ART LAYOUT DIRECTIONS

Step 1:   Design border or picture to go with page or pages of your part of the school almanac. Just sketch on regular paper first.

Step 2:   Once #1 is finished, make a decision as to where you want your artwork to go in relation to your writing that will be typed. Once you've decided where your artwork will go, roughly sketch it on paper (8½" by 11"), leaving a lot of space for the typing part of your project. This will be turned in to the typist with your writing, so she will leave appropriate space in relation to the typing for your artwork.

Step 3:   When typed page is complete, and you see *exactly* how much space is left for your picture,* draw it so it will fit on the typed page and to your liking on a separate piece of paper, cut it out, and glue it to typed page.

This method will eliminate typing over your page because you make a mistake with your artwork, or redoing your artwork because a typing error is made or there isn't enough room.

*Space size may change some because of allowance for typing. If typist can't allow enough space for artwork, should confer with writer, so appropriate changes can be made in writing or artwork.

Written copy
ready for typist

Space for
artwork

SCHOOL ALMANAC
(Possible ideas to be included)

1. School Bill of Rights and Amendments

2. School holidays and calendar year

3. Computer language and information about the school's computers

4. Association addresses students may want to write to

5. Study tips

6. Ways to earn money

7. School population and other statistics

8. Noted personalities of school (present and past)

9. Students' favorite TV shows, entertainers, food, etc.

10. Facts about city that school is in

11. Facts about community that school is in

12. Facts about taking care of pets

13. Information about the different classrooms

14. History of school and/or district

15. Most popular book, hero, etc.

16. Parent occupations

17. Information about organizations students may want to belong to

18. Colleges most students go to upon graduating from district's high school

UNIT III
STATE COLLAGE

- Categorizing state facts
- Research process
- Finding resources
- Validating research
- Drawing map true to scale
- Brainstorming symbols
- Light hookup

STATE COLLAGE — OVERALL PROJECT

The activities in this unit, besides being instructive and fun lessons within themselves, lead the student through the skills and processes he will need to know to complete the main project, that of the state collage, (see page 90) successfully.

Objectives, directions, and specific comments will be handled separately with each lesson. After each lesson (excluding lessons 1 and 2) students should work on that part of the requirements towards completion of the state collage. The following page is a student handout showing the specific requirements for the collage. The teacher may not want to hand it out until near the completion of the following lessons, so students don't become overwhelmed with what is expected of them—especially if they haven't been taught the how-to yet.

Students need to know where they are going, so the teacher should refer to a model collage (like on page 90) often where appropriate in lessons. The teacher should refer to the overall project on page 91 for directions on making it. Lessons in this unit will give even more specific directions if needed. Refer to the note cards on Hawaii on pages 112 to 116 and collage on page 90 for the symbols. The teacher's collage should be made with the same quality as is expected from the students. The teacher may end up enjoying making one as much as the students do. The light hookup should not be added to the teacher's, because it would stifle students' creativity in figuring out their own methods of hookup.

After students finish lesson on validating research, (pages 109-111), they need to pursue research on states of their choice and thus begin working towards a final project. Students need to finish one part of this project successfully before going to a second part—especially when it comes to validating research adequately before thinking up symbols and pictures for their collage and looking for them.

Students need a lot of individual time, once lessons have been given, to work on their individual projects. Since students all work at different speeds, time should be given to the students either in the classroom or at the library, so they can work on whatever stage they are at with their projects. Some of the work can be handled as homework as long as the teacher has a system to check to see that each student is progressing according to schedule.

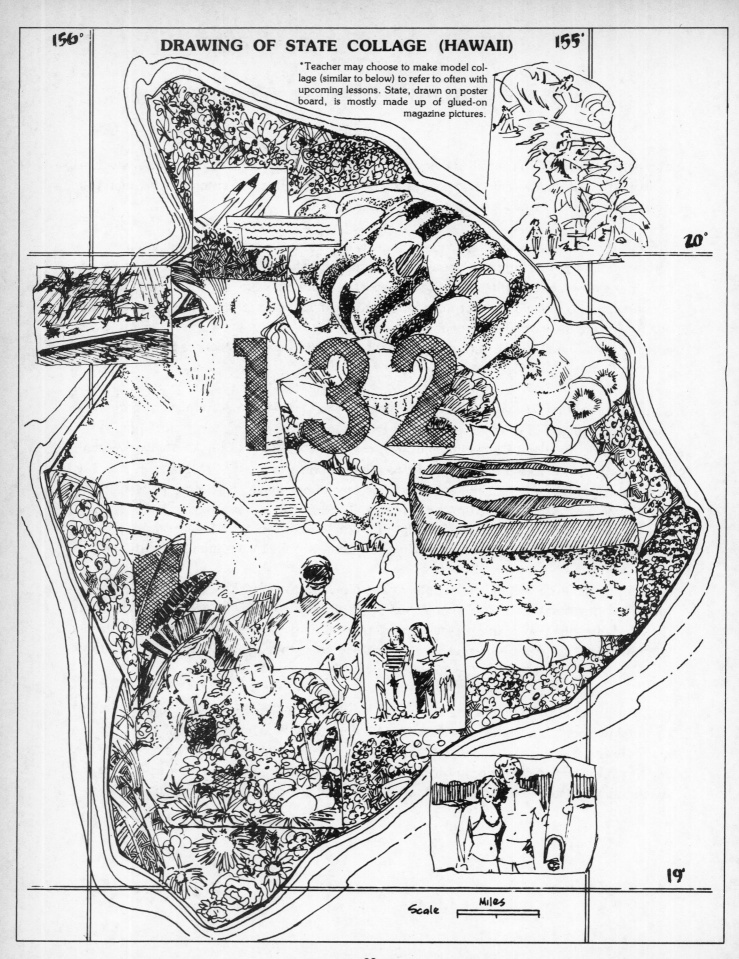

DRAWING OF STATE COLLAGE (HAWAII)

*Teacher may choose to make model collage (similar to below) to refer to often with upcoming lessons. State, drawn on poster board, is mostly made up of glued-on magazine pictures.

156°

155°

20°

19°

Scale   Miles

STATE COLLAGE—OVERALL PROJECT

Student Directions: The following things are requirements of the state collage assignment due on _____. You will receive instructions in each area ahead of time.

Teacher Directions: There will be more specific instructions in upcoming lessons.

1. Use the research process below to find information on your state.
    a. Think up questions you want to look up.
    b. List each question (category) on an index card that will be used to write down your answer.
    c. Locate resources where you will find your information.
    d. Look up answers to your questions in the resources.
    e. When you find information you want, write it on a card in as few words as possible. Put a symbol after the information to validate it. Cards may be checked by teacher.
    f. When you have gathered a satisfactory number of facts (many different symbols after the facts), then use the facts in your project.
2. Draw on heavy poster board a large outline of your state, true to scale, from a map of the state.
3. Draw in latitude and longitude lines where your state is located.
4. Brainstorm symbols of your facts that could be used on your collage. May use symbol webs on page 125.
5. Find pictures that symbolize the validated facts on your state.
6. Arrange cutout pictures within the outline you have drawn of your state. Overlap, cut, whatever you need, but fill in entire area within lines. Make sure you plan it carefully. When it has been planned carefully, and only then, glue pictures on.
7. Add light hookup to capital.
8. Add anything else that would add to the quality of your collage.

COMPARING STATE MAPS

Activity: Student will compare two states in the altas by interpreting their maps.

Material: 1. page 93 on STATE Y and STATE X
               2. paper, pencil
               3. string to measure perimeter to determine size
               4. atlas to find out what symbols stand for

Objectives: 1. Students will compare many things about states by looking at maps of
                  them.
               2. Students will interpret symbols on a map.
               3. Students will interpret climate by latitude.
               4. Students will look closely for detail on maps.

Directions: Students are to compare the two states on page 93 by studying the maps.
               They may need to refer to atlases for interpretation of symbols.

Comments: Students may not realize all the kinds of information which can be found on
               a simple state map. Asking them to compare the states makes them analyze
               what each state does and does not have. This activity encourages the use of
               the atlas as a resource for future use and also makes students more aware of
               some differences in states. Students should also be given same assignment
               but use real maps in atlases.

               If student has not been taught how to measure perimeter, see pages 15 to
               17.

92

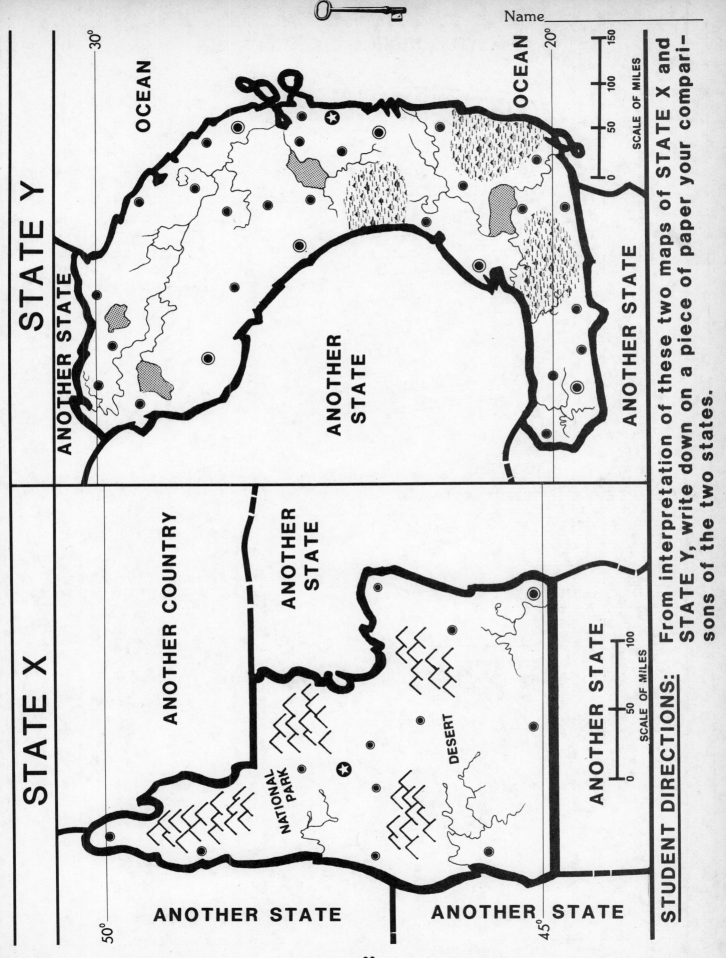

STATE Y

STATE X

OCEAN

OCEAN

ANOTHER STATE

ANOTHER STATE

ANOTHER STATE

ANOTHER
STATE

30°

20°

150

100

50

0

SCALE OF MILES

ANOTHER COUNTRY

ANOTHER
STATE

ANOTHER STATE

NATIONAL
PARK

DESERT

100

50

0

SCALE OF MILES

ANOTHER STATE

ANOTHER STATE

50°

45°

STUDENT DIRECTIONS: From interpretation of these two maps of STATE X and STATE Y, write down on a piece of paper your compari-sons of the two states.

93

CATEGORIZING STATE FACTS

CATEGORIZING STATE FACTS

Activity: Students will be led into activity of putting 100 state facts into categories that would be common research topics of states.

Material: 1. page 97 on definitions of state categories
2. pages 99 to 105 on state facts (Teacher may organize into game or station.)
3. dictionaries (optional)

Objectives: 1. Students will learn the first step in the research process (that of thinking up questions or categories) and then apply to their research for their collage.
2. Students will learn new vocabulary words pertaining to state attributes.
3. Students will put state facts into categories.

Directions:

Step 1:   The teacher shows collage model and explains that the pictures represent facts. The teacher then asks students how the teacher went about getting the information on the state. If students have not had much previous instruction with research, explain that the first step involves thinking up questions you want or need answered.

Ask students to come up with questions on states. Explain to them the questions should be categories of characteristics all states have, but that the characteristics of each category vary in each state. If students have difficulty with this, try these lead-in questions:

1. What makes up a state?
2. If you were going to move to another state, what types of things would you want to know about that state?
3. If you were doing research on a state, what kinds of information would you try to find?

What makes up a state?

What is the climate like?

Where is the state located?

Who are the inhabitants?

If continued difficulty, have students give information about the particular state they live in. The teacher lists information on board and organizes it into categories like below. The teacher may add or delete to meet his own personal needs.

Categories: Definitions and explanations of words are on page 97. After definition is given to students, students should have access to definitions for continual reference. Students may insert in own dictionaries.

agriculture/products   location

climate   natural resources

entertainment/recreation   topography

famous/special   tourist attractions

history   tradition

industry   vegetation

inhabitants

Explain to students the categories above really are questions because they ask for information. Ask students to state the question each one will ask if researching information on it.

Examples:

1. What is the **climate** like?
2. Who are the **inhabitants**?
3. Where is the state **located**?
4. What are some main **tourist attractions** of the state?

Step 2:   Pass list of definitions to students.

Step 3:   Pages 98 to 105 (STATE CATEGORY GAME)

DEFINITIONS AND QUALIFICATIONS OF STATE CATEGORIES*

*Teacher and/or students may prefer to come up with own definitions that all agree upon and resources validate.

1. Agriculture/Products: that which is produced from farming
2. Climate: the general weather conditions of a region (hot, humid, cold, dry, seasonal)
3. Entertainment/Recreation: play and amusement offered in state, which may not be necessarily offered in others. Michigan offers snow skiing, which can not be offered by all states.
4. Famous/Special: something important and unique from other states
5. History: something of importance to the United States' past—not just to the particular state even though it happened there
6. Industry: production and sale of products and services
7. Inhabitants: people or animals that live on the land (Examples in this book are of people.)
8. Location: simply where the state is in relation to other states, the world, latitude and longitude
9. Natural Resources: forms of wealth supplied by nature (ore, coal, oil)*
10. Topography: physical features of an area (mountains)
11. Tourist Attractions: things that people would travel to that state to see
12. Tradition: a set of customs unique to the state and passed down from generations
13. Vegetation: plant life of a region (tropical rain forest, coniferous forest, swamp, tundra)

*Teachers and/or students may broaden these definitions to meet their own needs. For example, timber could be included under natural resources, as well as under vegetation, if the definitions were broadened.

STATE CATEGORY GAME

Directions: After students feel comfortable with definitions on page 97, they are ready for this activity of categorizing state facts. Use pages 99 to 105 in one of four ways below.

1. As a written assignment, students would write what category the information falls under.
2. Teacher cuts facts, glues on index cards, and laminates. Either individual students or small groups place cards under which category the facts fall. There are three advantages to this if students work together. One, they learn from one another. Two, it gets away from the humdrum of writing out answers to everything. Three, it makes a nice station that can be fit into flexible slots of time.
3. A game could be set up by the teacher in which teams of individual students would get points for correct anwswers.
4. It could be easily computer programmed.

Note: The sentences found on pages 100 to 105 are typical of what you will find in different resources. When reading them, students need to decipher into what category they belong. The teacher may add more of his own choosing simply by researching through different resources and adapting information.

Comments: This activity is helpful for students because they frequently have difficulty deciphering information into categories when they do research on states.

Prior to this activity, the teacher can do a quick-review, categorizing game with the students. Number 2 above is popular. The dual purpose is to get students used to coming up with types of information that they will be looking for before they start research and then find the information in many resources to validate it.

STATE CATEGORY GAME

Student Directions: The categories below are some topic areas, in which you may find information about states. The following pages of sentences (cards) are the types of state facts you will find when doing research. Match the category each piece of information could go under (in some cases may fit into two).

AGRICULTURE/PRODUCTS	LOCATION
CLIMATE	NATURAL RESOURCES
ENTERTAINMENT/RECREATION	TOPOGRAPHY
FAMOUS/SPECIAL	TOURIST ATTRACTIONS
HISTORY	TRADITION
INDUSTRY	VEGETATION
INHABITANTS	

STATE CATEGORY GAME

1 The majority of Utah's land is suitable for grazing livestock.	**2** California ranks first among states in manufacturing.
3 Some chief crops of South Carolina are tobacoo, soybeans, cotton, and corn.	**4** There are many pictures of totem poles in books on Alaska.
5 Louisiana has many bayous (slow-moving inlets).	**6** The highest point in Florida is less than 400 feet.
7 Kentucky is the leading producer of coal.	**8** The major ethnic groups in New Mexico are Spanish, Indian, and English.
9 West Virginia has a lot of flash flooding.	**10** Florida's nickname is "The Sunshine State."
11 The Declaration of Independence and the Constitution were both signed in Philadelphia, Pennsylvania.	**12** Niagara Falls is in New York.
13 Rhode Island is ranked 50th in size.	**14** The museums in New York could give you your education.
15 President Reagan was the governor of California.	**16** South Carolina is between North Carolina and Georgia on the Atlantic Ocean.

STATE CATEGORY GAME

17 Crude petroleum, natural gas, sand and gravel production in 1979 was valued in the billions in Alaska.	**18** California's elevation ranges over 4,000 feet above sea level to hundreds of feet below sea level.
19 There are still dog sled races in Alaska.	**20** Wisconsin leads the nation in the production of milk, cream, butter, and cheese.
21 Brochures and books on Hawaii display many pictures of gorgeous flora growing all over Hawaii.	**22** Four seasons offer many recreation choices to Michiganians.
23 The Mormon's home base is in Salt Lake City, Utah.	**24** Ohio is "The Mother of Presidents."
25 California is approximately between 42°N latitude and 32.5°N latitude, offering much varied weather.	**26** North Dakota is covered with prairie grass.
27 Louisiana is known for its Dixieland jazz and Mardi Gras.	**28** Colorado has a lot of ski resorts.
29 Chinatown, near San Francisco, California, has the largest Chinese community outside of Asia.	**30** Madison Square Garden in New York offers everything from sport spectating to concerts to the public.
31 Walt Disney World is near Orlando, Florida.	**32** Michigan's two peninsulas are connected by the Mackinac Bridge.

STATE CATEGORY GAME

33 California is ranked first in population of all the states.	**34** Oregon's coast has mild to humid climate. In the interior there are extreme temperatures and more dryness.
35 California has very varied climate as a result of complex topography, wide latitudinal ranges, and ocean breezes.	**36** New Hampshire is generously covered with hardwoods and evergreens.
37 West Virginia is nicknamed "The Mountain State."	**38** Texas houses large deserts and endless plains.
39 New York still has reserves left of petroleum.	**40** There is textile manufacturing in Georgia.
41 Nebraska's nickname is "The Cornhusker State."	**42** In Georgia you'll find the Okefenokee Swamp, the largest preserved freshwater swamp in the United States.
43 Iowa has a record-breaking hog production.	**44** Rhode Island is the leading woolen manufacturing state.
45 On a map, Texas appears to have a lot of petroleum.	**46** Some of the major minerals mined in Utah are petroleum, copper, coal, gold, and uranium.
47 The United States Naval Academy is in Annapolis, Maryland.	**48** Considering New Jersey ranks 46th in size, it is densely populated.

STATE CATEGORY GAME

49 The industrial revolution began in Rhode Island.	50 Rhode Island is our smallest state.
51 Northern Michigan, a land of all seasons, offers almost every sport from skin diving to snow skiing.	52 Ohio has natural boundaries of Lake Erie and the Ohio River.
53 Most of Alaska has nearly 24 hours of daylight each summer.	54 Deserts with little vegetation cover a large portion of Utah.
55 New York houses the World Trade towers, the second tallest buildings in the world.	56 Looking at a map of Nevada, the state appears to have few county seats and cities.
57 Visitors are greeted with warm welcomes and leis in Hawaii.	58 Traverse City, Michigan, has long been known as the "Cherry Capital of the World."
59 Mountains as high as the Alps go through Washington.	60 There was a gold rush to California in 1849.
61 Florida's latitude is approximately between 25°N and 31°N.	62 Many Texans are proud to say they are cowboys.
63 Arizona is nicknamed "Grand Canyon State."	64 The Buffalo River in Arkansas offers great canoeing, fishing, and camping.

STATE CATEGORY GAME

65 New York is superior in manufacturing fields such as printing, publishing, and clothing.	**66** A map of Alabama shows the state has much cotton and peanuts.
67 New York surprisingly has a wealth of farmland.	**68** Textiles are South Carolina's most important industry.
69 Profits from farming in California are great.	**70** Michigan is surrounded by the Great Lakes.
71 There are many everglade symbols on a map of Florida.	**72** The Sea Islands off Georgia are warm-weather vacationers' dreams.
73 One of the worst recent volcanic eruptions in the States was Mt. St. Helens in Washington in May, 1980.	**74** In the winter the temperature in Chicago, Illinois, can go below 0° and in the summer rise to close to 100°.
75 During the Civil War, West Virginia split from Virginia, because it had more in common with the North.	**76** Indiana has four distinct seasons.
77 You'll find many hikers on the Appalachian Trail in Connecticut.	**78** Those interested in horses should enjoy the Kentucky Derby.
79 Oil refining is a big industry for Oklahoma.	**80** The Soo Locks at Sault Ste. Marie, Michigan, lift and lower boats 21 feet to the level of Lake Superior.

STATE CATEGORY GAME

81 Virginia has the Allegheny Mountains, Appalachian Mountains, and Blue Ridge Mountains all in her state.	**82** A map shows most of Florida's land is at sea level.
83 Sun Valley is a year-round resort in the Sawtooth Mountains of Idaho.	**84** The oldest living tree, 4600 years old, is in the Inyo National Forest in California.
85 Maine has popular coastal resort towns which offer a variety to water enthusiasts.	**86** On September 17, 1862, in Maryland, one of the bloodiest battles ever was fought at Antietam Battlefield.
87 A map shows a lot of trucking of vegetables takes place in Delaware.	**88** In Plymouth, Massachusetts, the first pilgrims settled in 1620 and celebrated their first Thanksgiving the following year.
89 Minnesota is bounded by Wisconsin, Lake Superior, Canada, the Dakotas, and Iowa.	**90** Missouri is susceptible to cold Canadian air and warm Gulf air.
91 Montana still has several Indian reservations covering millions of acres.	**92** Vermont leads states in production of maple sugar and syrup.
93 Tobacco is North Carolina's money crop.	**94** Mississippi has a semitropical climate with long summers and short winters.
95 South Dakota national parks offer hunting, camping, fishing, boating, skating, and skiing.	**96** Rhode Island is approximately between 40°N and 42°N latitude.

Answers on page 156.

RESOURCES

Activity: Students will become aware of all possible resources on information on states, gather, and use in their research for their state collage.

Material:
1. access to resources
2. resources
3. note cards
4. sample note cards, pages 112 to 116
5. colored pencils, pens, and/or crayons

Objectives:
1. Students will learn what different resources are available for their research.
2. Students will be resourceful by writing state Chamber of Commerce.
3. Students may learn correct business letter form.
4. Students will be resourceful by contacting a person familiar with the states of their choice.
5. Students will gain confidence by approaching other people regarding information they need.

Directions:
1. The teacher asks students what is the **first step** in the research process. A. Thinking of questions or topics which you want information on. Teacher then asks, "What do you do next?" A. "You look information up." Q. "Where?" A. "Places that have information." At this point teacher should lead into **third step*** of the research process—that of finding and locating these places of information called **resources** (may want to insert in dictionary). Teacher may have students brainstorm a list of resources that they may keep in their notes for reference.

Some valuable resources on states:

travel brochures	magazines
atlases	*National Geographic*
books on individual states	vertical file
books on United States	geographical dictionary
encyclopedias	person who's been there
almanacs	travel agent

***Second step** is setting up index cards properly which will be taught in next lesson. It doesn't matter which step comes first.

2. Ahead of time, have students write to the Chamber of Commerce of their states asking for information. Addresses are in most world almanacs. Most states will send information if you say you are planning to visit their "beautiful" state. However, not all students may receive information this way. That is why those that do receive such information should be allowed to share it with the class so others will see that being resourceful can pay off.

3. Have students give the names of states they and/or members of their families have become familiar with by visiting or living there. This should be logged somewhere by the teacher. It should be made clear that people who have lived in a state for some duration may be your best resource. The logged list becomes a list of valuable resources for the students to use accordingly:

   -Writing people who live in state of interest now and are not close enough to interview in person or by phone.
   -Interview in person or on phone other students or their relatives who have lived or visited in state of interest.

   A fun activity is to role play an interview situation in front of class. It will make students more comfortable when they do the real interview. This is one more way of being resourceful, and students should take notes on the information they receive. Page 108 will explain this part further.

4. Students will be taken to library and shown where most of their state resources are housed.

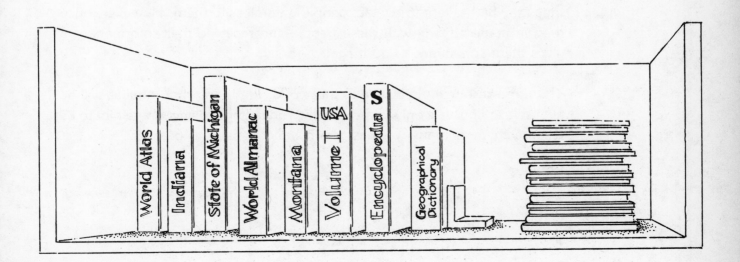

Extension: Explain to students once someone has thoroughly researched something, that he becomes a resource of that something (in this case a state.) Upon completion of students' state collages, have them fill out resource cards like below. They also can be filled out on states they've visited and/or lived in. Keep a file of the collected cards for classes in the future to use.

State

1. Resource Person: _____

2. Address: _____

3. Telephone #: _____

4. Place you can be a resource of: _____

5. What makes you a resource? _____

Comments: Many students may not be used to finding information on their own, other than what may be housed in the school library. They don't think of contacting other people outside of school and the home when they need information. Their world needs to be widened by making them aware of all the other resources available to them—in most cases right at their fingertips. At first, they may be hesitant to contact people unfamiliar to them. However, once they've made contact with these people and received their information, it gives them confidence to do it again.

The more resourceful you are in this world, the more opportunities will be available to you. It is only to the student's advantage to encourage him to be resourceful in as many ways as possible and as early as possible.

VALIDATING AND BEGINNING RESEARCH

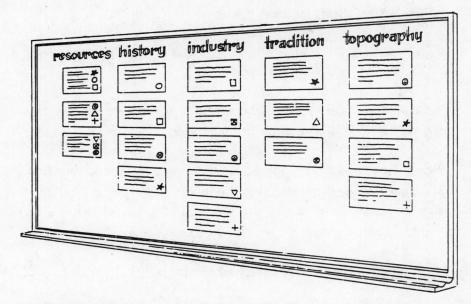

Activity: Students will learn a color-coding method to validate their research and use it when finding information for their state collages.

Material:
1. pages 112 to 116 on sample research cards on Hawaii
2. state collage model (Students may want to see where information on cards led.)
3. index cards
4. colored pencils, pens, and/or crayons
5. See **Optional** page 111 (many different resources on a state, paper used as magnified cards).

Objectives:
1. Students will learn and apply a way to validate their research.
2. Students will become aware that there is another step in the research process.
3. Students will prepare index cards for proper way of doing research on chosen states (pages 112 to 116).
4. Students will take down information correctly on chosen states.

Directions: Refer often to pages 112 to 116 for examples of steps 1 through 4.

Step 1: List resources you will be using on an index card. This will be your resource card. Think of a simple colored symbol to go with each resource similar to below.

Step 2: Place questions that you want to look up on top of index cards (one per card). For the purpose of the state research, a state category can be placed on top of each card. See page 97.

Step 3: Every time you write information down under a category, place the symbol by the information, indicating where you found it.

Example: "Pearl Harbor was attacked by the Japanese on December 7, 1941."

Your resource card will tell you what the symbol stands for. This stands for *The World Book Encyclopedia*.

Note: This would be a good time to remind students that they will be using symbols (pictures) to represent the facts that they find on their states, so they should just write down in the simplest way possible the information they want. Example could be shortened to:

"Japanese attacked Pearl Harbor 12/7/41."

Step 4: In most cases, if you find the same information in many different resources, the information is valid (true) and an important fact of that state. So before you accept all the information on the cards as true, you should have more than one symbol. Don't rewrite information you already found in another resource. Just add a new symbol to your original information, verifying you found the information somewhere else.

Example: "Japanese attacked Pearl Harbor 12/7/41."

The ⭐ symbol tells that the information was also found in *Academic America Encyclopedia*.

Step 5: Take students to the library and show them where all the resources for their projects are if they haven't been shown the previous lesson. Students are then ready to begin research with note cards. Spend as much time as seems necessary for students to feel comfortable with what they are to do. Students then can proceed on their own.

Optional: If students don't seem really comfortable with Steps 1 through 4, the class may choose to do some research together. The teacher may bring in volumes of resources on one particular state for students to plow through. Around the room he places magnified index cards with categories written on each one. With students, the teacher makes out a large resource card with all resources that the teacher brought in on it. The class can come up with symbols to represent each resource. Then the students try to find information on the state in the resources. When someone finds some information he goes to the card where he thinks the information belongs. If the class agrees it belongs on that card, then the student writes the information down. Before he marks down the symbol by the information, the class is to confirm if it is correct.

Comments: The first time students are taught the correct way to do research, a percentage of them do not delve into it with all kinds of enthusiasm. Research in itself is not always a student's favorite thing to do. Students like to know, but don't always like to take the time to find out. However, having a fun project such as the state collage gives a purpose for doing the research, and it becomes more motivating to students than learning the research process just for the sake of knowing it. And most students will not accept—"Well, you need to know it for later on."

Teacher persistence to see that the students follow through on their research as taught will definitely pay off in all future projects, besides the current one. Once students understand the research process, there usually are not complaints, and end products are much more in-depth and meaningful, and there definitely is no more regurgitation of that over-used encyclopedia. What once seemed a difficult task proves an easy task and a way of life.

A project with symbols (the kind on the state collage, not on the cards) can be designed to introduce note-taking and validating. Hopefully the students will not write complete sentences on their note cards, knowing they will not be writing sentences in reporting the information that they find.

Also, if students learn to think about what they are searching for in advance of their research, their notes should be simpler. Of course, there should be an allowance for developing new topics or questions as students think of new ideas while they are researching.

STATE COLLAGE EXAMPLE NOTE CARDS—HAWAII

Suggested Use: Run off for each student, or put on big cards, laminate, and display by collage of Hawaii.

front   back

Resources

1. The World Almanac △(g)*
2. Hammond Citation Atlas [b]
3. The Signet Hammond Atlas †
4. "Hawaii, The Aloha State" ○ brochure by State of Hawaii
5. Academic America Encyc. ☆

6. World Book Encyclopedia △(p)
7. The New Enchantment of America–Hawaii; Carpenter Allen, Children's Press; Chicago ☺
8. "Hawaii – It's more than a pretty place;" Hawaii Visitors' Bureau 1982

*Need to color code if you use the same symbol for different resources.

g = green   b = blue   p = purple

Agriculture / Products

- sugar (1st) △(g) ☺ □ ○ ☆ △(p)
- pineapples (2nd) △(g) ☺ □ ☆ △(p)
- macadamia nuts △(g) ○ △(p)
- fruits △(g) ○ ☆ △(p)
- coffee △(g) ○ ☆ △(p)

- vegetables △(g)
- melons △(g)
- beef cattle ☆ △(p)
- milk and dairy goods ☆ △(p)
- flora culture △(g) ○ ☆

*Since vegetables and melons were only found in one resource out of eight, they are not as important crops as the others and would not need to be included in the collage.

Climate

- temperate, mild △(p) ☺
- Mt. regions cooler △(g) ○ △(p) ☺
- enormous amount of rain – Mt. Waialeale, △(g) ☺ wettest spot in USA

- ideal year round □ △(p) between 70° and 80° ☺
- cooling trade winds ○ ☆ ○ △(p)
- between 19°N and 22°N △(p) †

112

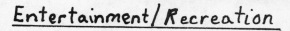

Entertainment / Recreation

- All nice weather sports ☐ ○ ⚠
- All ocean sports ☐ ○ ✦
surfing ☐ ○ ⚠ ☺
water tobogganing ☺
scuba diving ⚠ ✦
deep-sea fishing ⚠ sailing ⚠

- luaus ⚠ ☺
(with Hawaiian food + hula dancing)
- Polynesian Cultured Center ⚠ ✦
- snow skiing Mauna Kea ⚠
- hunting for game birds ✦

Famous / Special

- 50th state, Aug. 21, 1959 ⚠ ⚠
- In no other state life
expectancy so high ○ ☺
- Island of Kahoolawe ○
uninhabited target by ⚠
US Navy and Air Force ☺

- American defense center
in Pacific ○ ⚠
- Intercontinental satellite
network link in Pacific ○
- State was an independent
monarchy ☺ ⚠

*Since most of these Famous/Special facts have only one symbol, student would probably want to check other resources to validate.

History

- Bombing of Pearl Harbor ☺
Dec. 7, 1941 ○ ⚠ ⚠ ✦
(USS Arizona Memorial)
- youngest state ⚠ ✦
joined Union Aug. 21, 1959

- Queen Liliuokalani ✦ ⚠
was overthrown in ☺
1893 (end of monarchy)

Industry

- sugar refining ☺ △ ○ ☆ △
- fishing △ △
- canning pineapples ☆ △
- printed materials △ ☆
- stone △ ☆ △

- clay △ ☆
- glass products △ ☆
- clothing △ ☆ ☺
- lumber △
- oil refining ☺ ☆
- wood products △

Inhabitants

- ~~33%~~ white △ ☆ △ ☺
- ~~11%~~ black △ ☆ ☺
- ~~65%~~ Asian Americans ☆ △
  and Pacific Islanders △ ○ ☺
- ~~27%~~ Japanese ☆ △ △
- ~~14%~~ Filipino ☆ △ △

- ~~7%~~ Chinese ☆ △ △
- ~~9%~~ Hawaiian descent △
- American Indians ☆
- Hawaiian cowboys

*The exact percentages were crossed out, because the next resource contradicted these percentages.

Location

- in North Pacific, 2,397 mi.
  SW of San Francisco ☆ △ ☺
- between approx. 22° N and
  19° N +
- on the Tropic of Cancer ☆

- chain of 132 islands
  8 main ones, extends about
  1,600 miles △ ☆
- does not lie on mainland
  of U.S. △ ☆

Natural Resources

- few natural resources ☆
- bauxite ☆
- sand ☆
- limestone ☆
- gravel ☆

- stone ☆ △9
- clay ☆
- manganese ⎫ near ocean
- nickel ⎬ floor ☆
- copper ⎭
- petroleum ☆

*Obviously there are few natural resources in Hawaii—according to definition on page 97.

Topography

- Islands are tops of submerged mt. tops △9 △p
- active volcanoes ☺ △9 ☐ ○ △p +
- beaches ☐ △p
- cliffs ○ ☆ △9

- waterfalls ○ ☆ △
- about 130 islands ☆ ☺ △p
   - 8 sizeable ☆ △p
   - 7 inhabited ☆ ☺
- 132 islands △p

*One resource said about 130 islands; the other gave exact number. They validated one another thus the reason for the connecting arrow.

Tourist Attractions

- Tourism main source of income ○ ☆ ☺
- USS Arizona Memorial Pearl Harbor ☺ △ △ ☆
- volcanoes △ △9 ☺

- Diamond Head △9 ☺ ☆ △
- Waikki Beach △p △ ☆ ☺

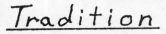

Tradition

- music, dancing (hula) from Polynesian melange culture ☺ □ ⚠
- l⎯⎯ (pig roast, feast dancing, + singing) ⚠ ☺

- leis ⚠ ☺ ▢r
- poi (root of taro plant used for this food) ⚠ ☺
- Hawaiian legend - volcanoes home of Pele the fire goddess ○ ☺

Vegetation

- thick growths of lush, green tropical plants, trees, and flowers □ ○ ⚠
- wooded areas at higher elevations ⚠
- tropical hardwoods + shrubs

- approx. 2,500 unique plants such as orchids, gardenias, + poinsettias ⭐☺
- edible plants + fruits ⭐☺⚠
- taro made into poi

MAKING MAPS TRUE TO SCALE

Activity: Students will learn to draw a large map of a state, true to scale, using a map in an atlas as a reference. The teacher makes available to students shapes and scales similar to those in different atlases, so students can practice drawing true to scale. This is a warm-up exercise to be done in preparation for drawing the state (collage) true to scale.

Material: 1. large paper (newspaper will suffice for warm-up)
2. markers, scissors, ruler, string, pencil
3. shapes like states on pages 119 and 120. The teacher should use pages by duplicating, cutting out, glueing on stronger backing, and laminating.
4. poster board or other backing for state collage. Wood may be used with the help of a carpenter.

Directions: *Teacher should demonstrate in front of room when teaching the following:

1. Students measure longest part of shape for length.
2. Students measure widest part for width.
3. Students measure width and length of large piece of paper.
4. Students multiply the width and length of shape by a number that will give new dimensions that will fit on the large piece of paper.
   Example: width of shape = 3"
              length of shape = 5"
              width of paper = 16"
              length of paper = 22"

If you multiplied the width and length of the shape by 4, you would have new dimensions of 12" by 20" which would fit on your paper.
5. Students make rectangles on their sheets the size of the new dimensions.
6. Students draw same shapes into rectangles.

Numbers 5 and 6:

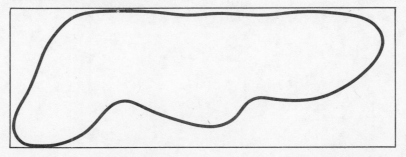

117

7. Once shape is drawn, figure out new scale of miles (see below). Whatever you multiplied your drawing by, you multiply your scale by.

Figuring out new scale:

1. Take a piece of string and measure the original scale from one end to the other. Then bend the yarn at the end of the scale. Fold it the number of times you multiplied your shape (state) by.

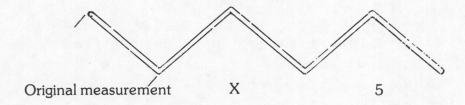

Original measurement   X   5

2. Stretch out the string straight, and draw a line with ruler the same length for your new scale.

3. Divide your new scale the same way the sample is. For example, if the halfway point is 50, put 50 at the halfway point of your new scale.

4. If scale needs to be divided into segments, students simply take a piece of yarn the same length as the scale and fold it into the number of segments needed. Then put a perpendicular line by each fold. Older students should be able to measure with ruler.

Comments: This can be a difficult task for students until broken down into the steps provided. With these steps, students find it challenging but not too complicated. After they have individually done the task cards made from pages 119 and 120, they are comfortable enough to apply the skill to their state collages.

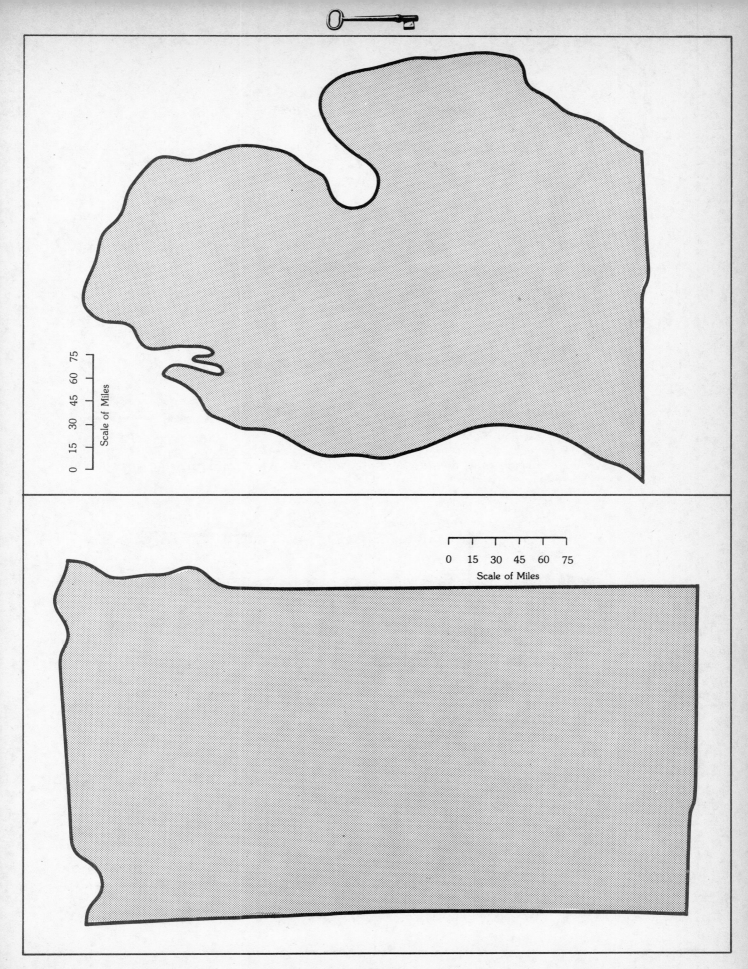

Scale of Miles

0 15 30 45 60 75

0   15   30   45   60   75
Scale of Miles

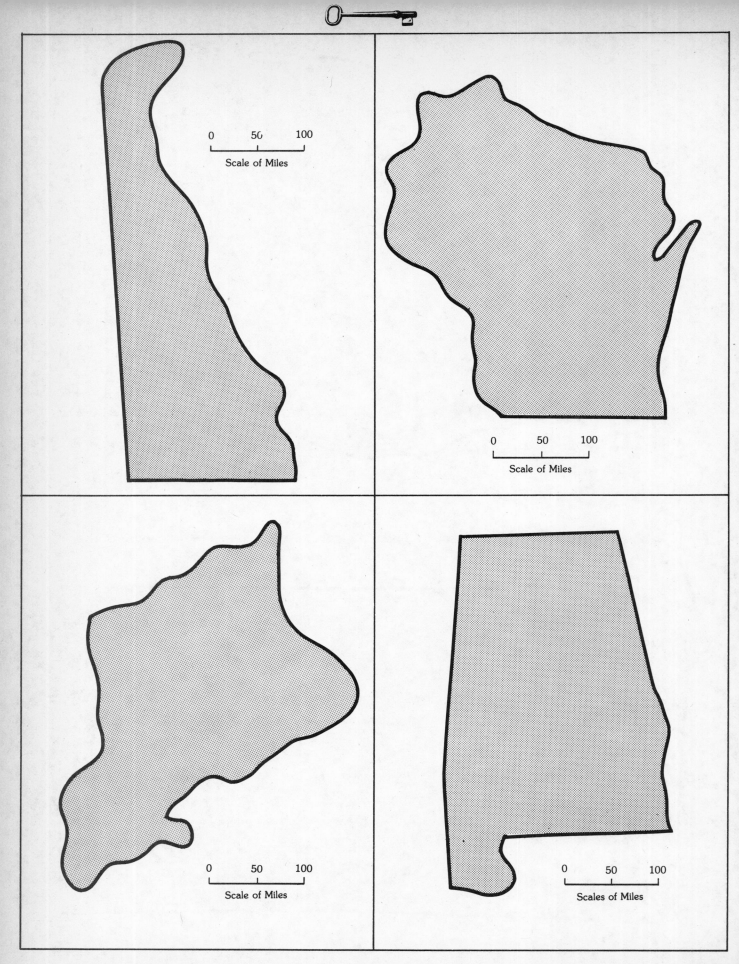

0   50   100
Scale of Miles

0   50   100
Scale of Miles

0   50   100
Scale of Miles

0   50   100
Scales of Miles

BRAINSTORMING SYMBOLS

Activity: Students brainstorm ways of symbolizing the facts on their states.

Material: 1. model collage on Hawaii (similar to page 90) or other state if teacher chooses
              2. chalkboard
              3. pages 123 to 125 in this book
              4. note cards with state facts on them (See pages 112 to 116.)
              5. magazines

Objectives: 1. Students will be creative in coming up with pictures to represent factual information.
              2. Students will analyze relationships/associations between things.
              3. Students will find all pictures for their collages.

Directions:
Step 1:   The teacher brings out collage of Hawaii and discusses the meaning of the different symbols.

              1. 132 stands for number of islands Hawaii has.
              2. Cake represents sugar cane, a main product.
              3. Rockets stand for bombing of Pearl Harbor.
              4. Fire stands for the volcanoes that Hawaii is made up of.

              Explain that these symbols (pictures in most cases, but do not have to be) in some way depict the meanings relevant to the facts (which have been validated).

Step 2:   The teacher explains to students that they are going to come up with ways of representing state facts. On chalkboard teacher writes down an important fact of a state. She may choose to take one from page 123 in this book. Explain to students that they are ready to start finding pictures that could go with the fact on the board. Either draw or write students' ideas at end of web strings. Ask students why they chose their ideas. There has to be an association with the fact! Teacher may add her ideas or ideas from page 124 to stimulate thoughts from students.

Step 3: When students seem to understand Steps 1 and 2, pass out fact webs from page 123.
Give them quiet think time to come up with as many associations as possible. At the end of comfortable time for you, let students share ideas.

Step 4: Pass out page 125 to students to use for the facts on their states. Tell them to use these for more difficult facts or ones they think may be hard to find something on in the magazines. Products, for instance, are not too difficult in that you can either find a picture of the raw product (apple) or something made from it (juice, pie). The teacher should also explain that sometimes going through magazines and seeing all kinds of pictures of things may give you more ideas.

Step 5: After students have come up with many ideas on how to represent their facts, have them have fun going through magazines to find pictures. This may be done at home.

Comments: Finding pictures to represent factual information is the perfect opportunity to challenge students to brainstorm all possible associations—to stretch their brains. It probably goes without saying, that because of this activity, students' collages are a lot more creative than the collages of students who did not have this activity.

BRAINSTORMING SYMBOLS

Student Directions: Either cut out or draw pictures at the end of the web strings that could symbolize the information below.

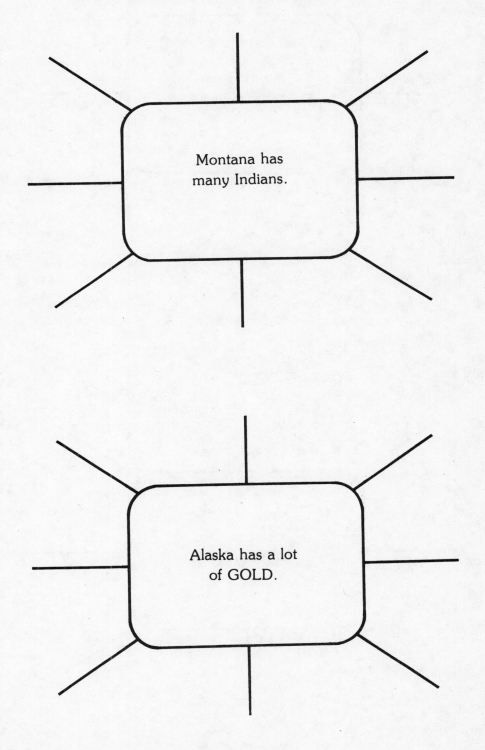

Montana has many Indians.

Alaska has a lot of GOLD.

BRAINSTORMING SYMBOLS—Possible Answers

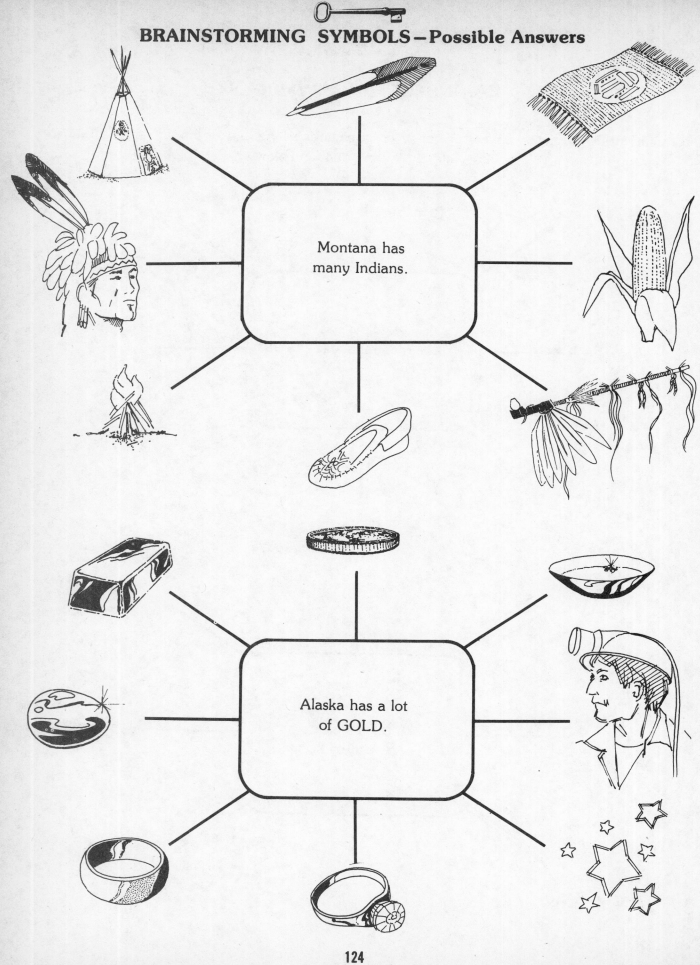

Montana has many Indians.

Alaska has a lot of GOLD.

BRAINSTORMING SYMBOLS

Student Directions: Write down factual information on your state in the squares and cut out or draw pictures at the end of the strings that could symbolize the fact.

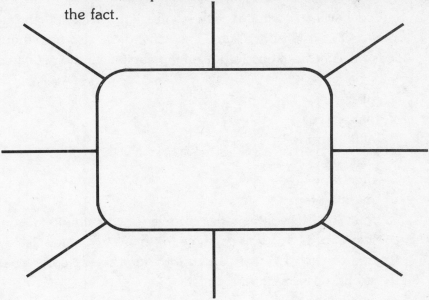

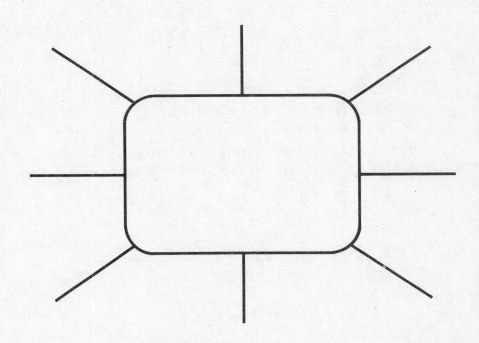

LIGHT HOOKUP

Activity: Students will experiment with conducting electricity through closed and open circuits to produce light. The activity will also help them come up with ideas for light hookups (representing capital) to their state collages.

Material:
1. pliers
2. paper clips
3. aluminum foil
4. bell wire
5. duct tape
6. masking tape
7. four AA 1.5 volt batteries for every two students or station
8. two C or D 1.5 volt batteries for every two students or station
9. one dry cell 1.5 volt battery for every two students or station
10. strong scissors or wire cutters
11. small light bulb

Note: If these items are not available in home workshop, they are available in most hardware stores.

Objectives:
1. Students will learn about the conduction of electricity.
2. Students will invent a way to hook up a light that may be turned off and on and attach it to their collages.
3. Students will learn about open and closed circuits.
4. Students will have experience testing their hypotheses on what will make the bulb light up.

Directions: The teacher turns on the light in class, and asks students why they think the light went on. Most of them, at least, should mention something about electricity. The teacher forms questions by students' responses (R) and leads students into the discussion of closed circuits (definitions on page 129). A diagram similar to below on the board may help with understanding.

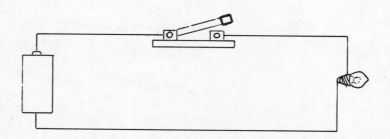

If students seem to have no background on this, show them a simple example with a dry cell battery, wire, and light bulb (like example A on page 130). The teacher continues asking questions (Q).

Q. "What do you think will happen when we close the circuit?" R. "Electricity will continually flow round and round. The filament in the light bulb will get so hot it will glow." Q. "What will happen if we open the circuit?" R. "The connection will be broken, and there will be no light."

The teacher needs to make sure students understand the following concepts before proceeding:

1. The wire conducts the electricity.
2. One end of circuit has to connect + positive end of battery, and other end has to connect − negative end of battery. Let students find positive and negative ends.
3. About 1" insulation has to be removed from wire before connection.

Next, the teacher tells the students they will be experimenting with the materials available to see how many ways they can come up with to turn the light on and off easily. This should lead them to devise ways to hook up lights (that may be turned on and off) to their state collages where the state capitals are.

It will be more economical if students work with partners. It may even be necessary for four to six students to share materials, which could easily be set up at a station. When students come up with a solution, they draw a diagram of it to be shared later. It is the teacher's responsibility to walk around and help the students come up with solutions similar to those found on pages 130 and 131. This can be done by asking questions that begin like, "What would happen if...?"

Students share diagrams, with their own explanations, at the end of the lesson.

Comments: The requirement of the light hookup as a part of the collage assignment can be a challenge to students. The teacher may choose to have them experiment with hookup solutions on their own before asking them to figure out how to attach them to their collages.

Students may have to purchase some materials, and it should be made clear that not all the equipment they work with at the stations is necessary. Challenge them to come up with inexpensive ways of doing things. The teacher should have extra light bulbs, batteries, and wire available for anyone who can't acquire it through the home. The items needed would be good donations to ask for at the beginning of the year from parents and companies in your town.

This light hookup is a very successful way of bringing science into the state collage project. When students explain their final finished projects, they will seldom leave out how the lights work.

If a student becomes extremely absorbed in the concept of electricity and the experimentation of the light hookup, encourage him to be resourceful and find books on the subject and allow him opportunities to share new experiments in front of his class.

LIGHT HOOKUP

Vocabulary Words

*Students may want to insert in dictionaries.

1. Circuit: a path for electricty

2. Open Circuit: an incomplete or broken path for electricity

3. Closed Circuit: a complete or unbroken path for electricity

4. Conductor: something that transmits electricity

5. Electricity: current used as a source of power

6. Experiment: test used to prove if hypothesis is valid

7. Filament: thin connecting wire in light bulb

8. Hypothesis: an explanation that can explain a reason why and be tested to be true or false by investigation and experimentation

LIGHT HOOKUP

There are various possibilities of producing light that can be turned on and off. Students may make any combination of examples.

A.

A. One end of wire #1 has been coiled around screw part of light bulb. Other end has been connected to dry cell. #2 wire has been connected to dry cell. When you touch other end of wire to light bulb, you will close the circuit, and the light bulb will go on.

B.

B. One end of wire #1 has been coiled around screw part of light bulb. Other end has been attached by duct tape to end of C battery. #2 wire is attached to positive end of second battery by duct tape. Duct tape has been wrapped around two batteries and ends of wires to hold them all in place. Other end of wire #2 is attached to a paper clip (a conductor). One end of wire #3 is attached by tape to bottom of light bulb. When end of wire #3 is connected to paper clip, the circuit will be closed, and the bulb will light up.

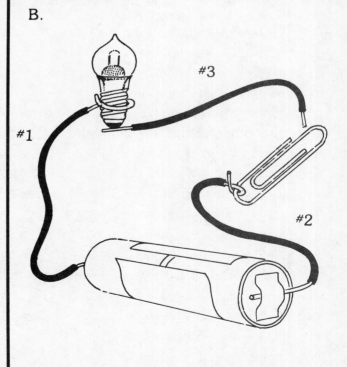

C.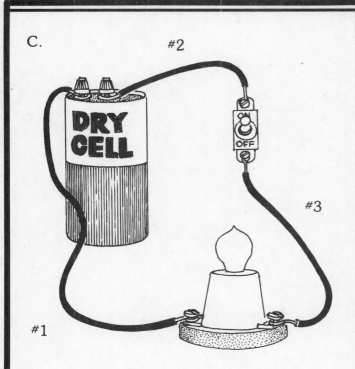

#2

#3

#1

C. Light bulb has been inserted into light socket. One end of wire is attached to socket and other end to dry cell. Wire #2 is attached to dry cell and wire of on-and-off switch. Wire #3 is attached to wire of on-and-off switch and socket.

D. Wire #1 is attached to socket and group of four AA batteries (1.5 volts each) by duct tape. The batteries are also held together with duct tape. All positive ends of the batteries face one way and negative ends the other. Strips of aluminum foil have been placed along the negative end and the positive end, and the ends of the wire are actually touching the strips of foil. They act as conductors. Wire #2 is attached to other end of batteries, and tip of wire (insulation removed) is used as an on-and-off switch. Wire #3 is attached to socket, and tip of wire is used as an on-and-off switch. When you connect wires #2 and #3, you close the circuit, and the light will be switched on.

D.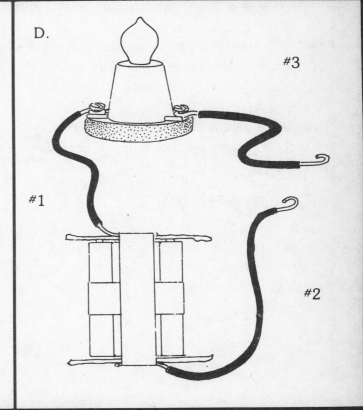

#3

#1

#2

Shown below is one of the easiest, lightest, and least expensive ways of hooking up a light to the state collage.

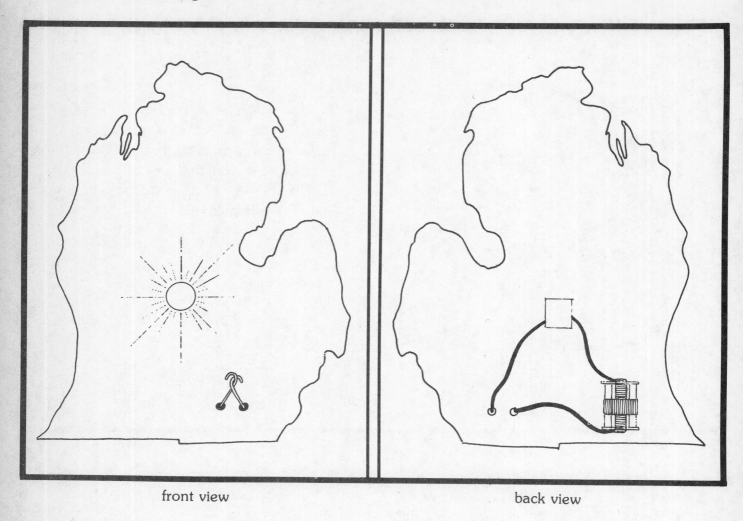

front view   back view

This is like example D, except the light is not in a socket. A crossed slit (+) is made with an X-acto knife in the poster board to hold the light bulb. Two small holes are made for the ends of wire to stick through to the front side to act as connectors. Everything is securely taped on with duct tape.

UNIT IV
USING ALL WORLDLY RESOURCES

- PEN PALS
- TRAVEL BROCHURES

Oregon
the beaver state

Pacific Ocean

Portland

the World Atlas

the World Almanac

USA

USA

EXAMPLE OF A PEN PAL LETTER

Dear Pen Pal,

My name is Kim Kato-san. I am 11 years old. I live with my sister, 14, and my mother and father in Yokohama, Japan. It is a very large city (over 2,600,000 people), 20 miles south of Tokyo, which is one of the world's largest cities. If you want to look up where I live on a map, it is around 35°N and 140°E.

My father repairs very big ships that carry imports and exports in and out of our country by way of the Pacific Ocean and the Sagami Sea.

I have three terms of school a year: January to March; April to July; and September to December, with vacation time in between. I work very hard at my studies. I have to so I will pass the exam when I am 15 that will allow me to attend the high school. There are 38 students in my sixth-grade classroom right now. We all respect our teacher very much.

During my vacation time, I play a little baseball, watch TV, do homework, and window-shop. Someday I want to buy a computer very much. In the summer I go to the beach with my family on weekends. Sometimes we go on picnics around the city. The biggest event of the year that we all spend a lot of time preparing for is New Years. It lasts for three days. I, also, have to run errands for my mother and work in our family garden.

Please tell me all about your family, your country, your school, and what you do for fun. I'd also like to know all about the customs and traditions of your country that you and your family participate in. In my next letter, I will tell you all about ours.

I'm looking forward to hearing from you.

Respectfully yours,

Kim Kato-san

PEN PALS

Activity: Students become pen pals from other countries and research their countries for information that will help with their writing.

Material: 1. same type writing paper and envelopes for each student
               2. international mailbox
               3. atlas and other world resources

Objectives: 1. Students will learn about different countries in the world.
               2. Students will realize that the place someone lives in the world influences his lifestyle.
               3. Students will understand another culture.
               4. Students will look up in different resources information on countries they are from to answer questions of pen pal.
               5. Students will put factual information into letter form.
               6. Students will be creative in their portrayal of fictitious characters.
               7. Students may appreciate their own culture more.

Directions:

Step 1:   1. The teacher explains to students that they all will become fictitious students from other countries of their choice. Each student will make up a letter about his life in that country based on facts of the country and place his letter in an international mailbox. The teacher will deliver his letter to the appropriate pen pal. All the letters and envelopes written should be on paper the teacher gives, so it will be harder to guess who is whose pen pal.

               2. The teacher asks each student to brainstorm things he would need or want to know about a pen pal, living in a different country, such as age, name, address, family, hobbies, parents' jobs, school routine, types of houses, types of food, customs, current news of the country, the country's government, country's climate, country's landscape, and tourist attractions.

               3. The teacher tells students that they will all write one letter first without knowing who their pen pals are to be. It will all be made up except for their being students, but the letters must be based on true facts of the country each chooses to be from. Each letter should be as authentic as if the student was living in the country.

4. The teacher may choose to read the letter from Kim Kato-san on page 141, so students will get a better idea of what is expected.

5. The teacher should also have class give all possible countries pen pals could be from, using an atlas. This is so students will be more diversified in their selection.*

Step 2:   The teacher has resources about different countries available for students to plow through to help them with their decisions on countries they want to be from.
examples:

atlases	encyclopedias
almanacs	*National Geographic*
newspaper articles	movies of countries
magazine articles	filmstrips of countries
books on the world	books of countries

By the end of a specified period of time, the student should tell the teacher, and only the teacher, his assumed name and what country he will be from.

Step 3:   Students research the area of their choice. Area should be narrowed down to the size of a city. Note cards should be used as taught on pages 109-116.

Step 4:   An international mailbox needs to be made. It may be made by the teacher or group of students. The teacher should at least provide a large cardboard box with a slit in it. It could simply be wrapped with white paper, and stenciled letters "INTERNATIONAL MAILBOX" glued on. Or it may be decorated any way the teacher and students see fit.

Step 5:   Each student writes his introductory letter, not knowing who his new pen pal will be. All letters are put in the international mailbox. The teacher gathers them and disperses them to students. The letter each student receives is from his pen pal—except, of course, if student receives his own, in which case the teacher would take it back and hand over another one. The teacher has the option of pairing up certain students to be pen pals if she prefers.

*Teacher may choose to have students select from pieces of paper, with a different country on each one, to determine students' countries.

Step 6:   At another designated time, students answer the letters received from their pen pals, and again, mail them in the international mailbox.

Ongoing communication takes place at the discretion of the teacher. Structured time should always be there for this purpose. (If students want to write at other times too, this may be allowed if it does not interfere with regular assignments.) It is suggested prior to each time set aside, the teacher go over some good types of pen pal writing. The teacher should also explain to students that questioning pen pals about the life in their countries may lead to more informative letters from them. Remember to always have available for students an adequate number of resources, and they must be available for use prior to each letter designed by the student.

Step 7:   At the end of the unit (after several letters or a specified time, whatever the teacher decides) it should be time for students to find out who their pen pals really are. An international party would be fun where each student dresses up like the person he has been portraying. Students may want to bring in samples of food from their countries. The class may want to invite other rooms.

During the festivities, students may find their pen pals and introduce them to the group. They may bring up some important things about them and the lives they led.

Alternative: Two classes could also exchange pen pals. This is much easier, to keep pen pals' true identities secret. Students within a room could share where they and their pen pals are from, but discussion of it should remain in the room. In this case, each class would have an international mailbox unless the classes were held in the same room at different times. With this alternative, letters should be shared.

Comments: There should be as much guidance from the teacher as needed in this assignment. The teacher should make sure students have researched their area well before attempting to portray a person living there.

The teacher needs to challenge their creativity by making sure they take the facts and incorporate them into interesting letters that real pen pals would write. With each new letter each pen pal writes and receives, added interest in the countries should be evident and more research needed.

This assignment is most successful when classes exchange letters, and the teacher selects who will be whose pen pal. When the classes that exchange letters have different numbers of students in them, something has to be done to even up the numbers. Students, in the smaller class volunteering to have two pen pals, easily solve the problem. Also, the teacher can become a pen pal. When small classes (up to 12) exchange letters, each student could read one well-written paragraph to the group from his pen pal. It should be informative, yet written as a pen pal might really write it. Two good paragraphs from Gopal, a little boy who lives in a farming village in India, are below.

> You may be able to smell the fish I had for dinner in this letter. I haven't been to the canal yet to wash my hands. I'll do that on the way to delivering this letter to someone who will take it to the city for me. I need to go out and find a new mango twig anyway. The one I have doesn't clean my teeth very well anymore.

> Too bad I didn't have this letter with me yesterday. Father and I took the ox cart and went to the city to sell the saris that Grandfather makes to a shop. By the way, a sari is a long piece of dyed cloth (25 ft.) that a woman wraps around her waist and then throws over her shoulder. My mother owns a couple of cotton ones and a silk one for holidays and going to the temple.

PEN PALS

Dear Pen Pal,

My name is Kim Kato-san. I am 11 years old. I live with my sister, 14, and my mother and father in Yokohama, Japan. It is a very large city (over 2,600,000 people), 20 miles south of Tokyo, which is one of the world's largest cities. If you want to look up where I live on a map, it is around 35°N and 140°E.

My father repairs very big ships that carry imports and exports in and out of our country by way of the Pacific Ocean and the Sagami Sea.

I have three terms of school a year: January to March; April to July; and September to December, with vacation time in between. I work very hard at my studies. I have to so I will pass the exam when I am 15 that will allow me to attend the high school. There are 38 students in my sixth-grade classroom right now. We all respect our teacher very much.

During my vacation time, I play a little baseball, watch TV, do homework, and window-shop. Someday I want to buy a computer very much. In the summer I go to the beach with my family on weekends. Sometimes we go on picnics around the city. The biggest event of the year that we all spend a lot of time preparing for is New Years. It lasts for three days. I, also, have to run errands for my mother and work in our family garden.

Please tell me all about your family, your country, your school, and what you do for fun. I'd also like to know all about the customs and traditions of your country that you and your family participate in. In my next letter, I will tell you all about ours.

I'm looking forward to hearing from you.

Respectfully yours,

Kim Kato-san

TRAVEL BROCHURES

TRAVEL BROCHURES

Activity: The teacher will go over with students the putting together of information about a state into a travel brochure that convinces others to travel to that particular state. Then students will individually go through the process and design a brochure of a state of their own choosing.

Material: 1. resources on states
             2. travel brochures
             3. paper
             4. materials for drawing
             5. typewriter (optional)

Objectives: 1. Students will learn about different states.
             2. Students will learn about different resources.
             3. Students will use a thesaurus.
             4. Students will use writing skills to convince someone to travel to a state.
             5. Students will come up with many descriptive words to help describe what various states offer.
             6. Students will plan ahead an end product.

Directions:

Step 1:   Students should brainstorm questions/categories that need researching for travel brochures. The teacher needs some lead-in questions similar to below. Questions will vary according to reactions and responses (R) of students. The information in the elicited responses below is important for the students to know before proceeding to Step 2.

Q. What is the first step when doing research on something? (If haven't had it, refer back to page 95.)

R. Thinking of questions or categories of information you need to find information on.

Q. Now we're going to design travel brochures. What's a travel brochure?

R. A travel brochure is a pamphlet or small booklet giving information about a place to visit. The purpose of most brochures is to help convince people to come to the area the brochure is advertising. (This is a good time to show various brochures.)

Q. So for the most part, you are going to advertise an area, for this assignment—a state. What questions about the state do you need answered first? What questions are you interested in having answered before you choose to travel somewhere?

It is important the preceding questions lead into similar responses below.

1. Where is it located?
2. What is the climate like?
3. What scenery is worth seeing?
4. What sports are offered?
5. What tourist attractions are there?
6. Is there anything unusual about the state that would give people reason to visit it?
7. What types of entertainment are offered?

Step 2:   The teacher explains that for their final project of a travel brochure on a state of their own choosing, students will have to research the above questions. They may do this like pages 109-116. But right now, each student is to answer these questions on his own state. Students should be reminded they are resources of their own states, because they live there. Resources on the states should be available though, so students can snoop through. Some students may be new in the state and/or haven't traveled much in their own state.

After students have had time to discuss questions and look through materials, students give answers to questions 1 through 7. Michigan is used throughout this activity as an example. Some examples of students' answers are as follows:

Location: upper part of the United States surrounded by four Great Lakes

Climate: seasonal: winter, spring, summer, and fall

Scenery: forests, change of seasons, lakes, beaches, tulips

Sports: all seasonal: summer—swimming, golfing, tennis, dune rides, boating; winter—snowmobiling, skiing, ice skating, hockey

Entertainment: (may choose to leave out)
                In bigger cities like Grand Rapids, Lansing, Traverse City, and Detroit: museums, zoos, Pontiac Stadium (Detroit Lions), Tigers' Baseball Stadium, dining places, all sport facilities, and all kinds of festivals (ethnic, art, Coast Guard)

Tourist Attractions: (should be unique to state—see definition on page 97.)

1. Mackinac Island—island by Straits of Mackinac on which there are no cars allowed and plenty of horse drawn carriages.
2. Greenfield Village and the Henry Ford Museum—history will come alive for you. The first car was invented here.
3. Soo Locks at Sault St. Marie lower to Lake Huron or Lake Superior allowing ships to pass through.
4. Tahquamenon Falls in upper penninsula—largest of 150 falls and frozen in winter
5. Holland Tulip Festival—in spring millions of different colored tulips are displayed artistically in gardens for tourists to visit. Ethnic festivities go on for a week.
6. Gerald Ford Museum in Grand Rapids
7. clean beaches and lakes throughout Michigan

Anything Unusual: It has a lower and upper penninsula. Upper Penninsula has not been developed much, so its beautiful, untouched wilderness and water holds much for tourists. Michigan was named Michi-Gama meaning "Land of Lakes" by Indians.

Step 3: Students should go back to information gathered and come up with reasons why people would want to travel to their states because of the information. For example, if you were doing Florida and were discussing its warm yearly climate, you certainly wouldn't mention that people would miss snow at Christmas or that they couldn't go snow skiing. You'd only mention the positive things of being warm all year. The teacher may choose to go over total brainstormed list and have students discuss all the positive effects.

Step 4: The teacher needs to reiterate that the biggest challenge of this assignment is to convince the reader he should travel to the state. When convincing others of something, it is important what words you select because this is a very challenging means of communication. At this point, the teacher may want to read some good writing from travel brochures. Then ask the students what words helped them picture in their minds the wonderful parts of the state.

Students need to think of descriptive words before their actual writing. Words have to help describe what is going on in the state. They need to create imagery through all the senses. Once students seem to realize the importance of words, have them brainstorm words to describe some nouns that really reflect the state as was done on page 150. Use a thesaurus* when list seems exhausted.

Step 5:   Decide on organization of brochure.
1. When writing, have a plan on how you are going to tie all the information in before actual writing.
    Examples with Michigan:
    a. separate section on different seasons and what each season has to offer (Brochure on pages 148 and 149 was set up like this.)
    b. separate sections on climate, scenery, tourist attractions, sports, history, etc.
    c. what a weekend would be like in state—take reader on an imaginary trip (morning, noon, night of each day)
    d. combination of above ideas
    e. Have students come up with more ideas.

2. Decide how you are going to fold your paper, and where your pictures are going to go. Pictures can accent writing or be a form of communication themselves. In the brochure on page 148, the pictures on the map of Michigan convey many of the tourist attractions around the state.

Paper-folding possibilities:

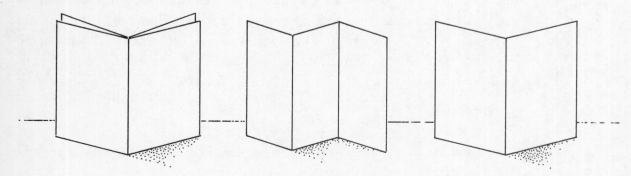

*A thesaurus is a book of similes and related words.

Step 6:   Once students seem to have a plan, they can write and add artwork to their brochures. The gathered information and descriptive words should be in front of them. After a certain amount of time, students may share their products with each other. This is mainly to get them excited with the project and to feel confident in pursuing it on their own.

Step 7:   Individual final project: For the final project in which the student will follow the same steps above, only individually, much more care should be taken. Pictures should be drawn on separate paper and glued on. The writing should also be done this way. The final writing (after editing, if teacher chooses) would look best on lined paper glued on or typed.

It is up to the teacher if he wants to provide resources from which students can gather information. Good resources are books, magazines, travel brochures, travel guides, atlases, almanacs, encyclopedias, a geographical dictionary. However, by now, students should be able to find and use them well on their own. To make sure all students have fair access to these materials, a trip to the library may be necessary with teacher supervising note-taking.

If the teacher checks over information gathered, students' lists of descriptive words, plans of design, and actual writing, the brochures should be of high quality. When brochures are finished, they should be shared and displayed.

Again, it is up to the teacher how much classtime is used for the project and how much is to be done as homework, if any.

Comments: A plan which usually works well is to take students to the library to do their research. When their research is completed, assign the rest of the project as homework. The teacher needs to keep a check on individual progress.

If students are to produce brochures of high quality, especially where the writing is concerned, it is important they follow the steps listed. It is the same story heard throughout this book—a good end product takes know-how, planning, and thorough follow-through of all possible steps leading to the end product.

Students enjoy this activity immensely, and beautiful and creative brochures can be displayed on a bulletin board for all to enjoy.

SAMPLE TRAVEL BROCHURE

FRONT
TOP

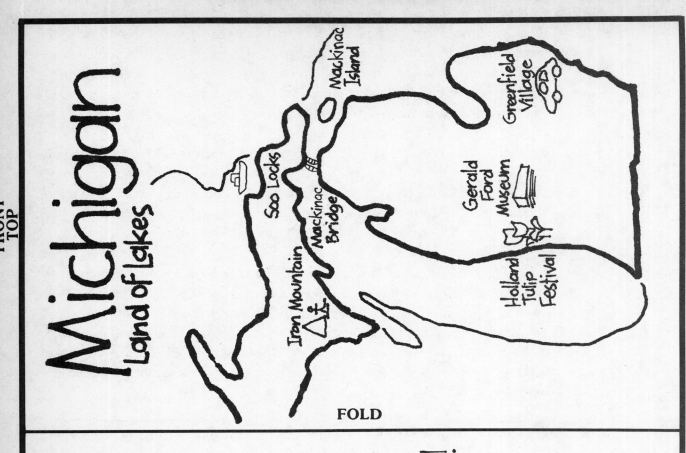

Michigan
Land of Lakes

Mackinac Island

Greenfield Village

Soo Locks

Mackinac Bridge

Gerald Ford Museum

Holland Tulip Festival

Iron Mountain

FOLD

BACK
TOP

Most everyone wants snow for Christmas, and Michigan offers tons of it. Along with its small mountains are ski resorts throughout Michigan. It is so relaxing after a refreshing cool ski run to come into one of their rustic lodges and enjoy the warmth and glow of a roaring fire. Or if you prefer, continue enjoying the invigorating outdoors of Michigan by snowmobiling, ice skating, ice fishing or even making a snowman.

Whatever you want, Michigan has it, and it's waiting for you. So come soon. Come visit Michigan!

Directions: Duplicate pages 148 and 149 cut, and fold.

Spring gently develops into summer and then offers fun, fun, fun along the shores of its hundreds of lakes. There is something for everyone: swimming, golfing, tennis, fishing, and dune rides. For the romanticist there can be cool walks along the beaches at night and the listening to the gentle waves rolling in. Hundreds of elegant places wait to be dined and danced in.

Fall offers a kaleidoscope of colors with the changing of the leaves. As you travel north through Michigan, the yellows, oranges, and reds are accented by the emerald-blue waters and dark green forests.

The Indians named Michigan "Michi-Gama," meaning Land of Lakes because it is surrounded by some of the world's largest lakes, which offer beauty and fun to all those that visit. Michigan is in the upper part of the United States, and thus has the advantages of what four climates can offer you.

In the spring there is the breathtaking beauty of the snow melting and the land giving birth to blossoms and greenery. A main attraction in the spring is the Holland Tulip Festival, which displays thousands of colorful arrays of tulips.

TRAVEL BROCHURES—DESCRIPTIVE WORDS

(brainstormed and found in thesaurus by author's students)

TULIPS	WATER
colorful, vivid, bright	clean, clear, transparent
rainbow hued, rainbowy	crystal clear, glassy
medley of colors	gleaming, glistening, sparkly
red, yellow, pink, white	blue, turquoise, emerald
many hued, vari-colored	cool, tingling, refreshing
kaleidoscopic, prismatic	tantalizing, breathtaking
polychromic, in technicolor	zesty, stimulating, invigorating
BEACHES	**LEAVES (fall)**
shore, lakeside	*Same words for tulips
fun, entertaining, amusing	red, scarlet, cardinal
recreational, sensational	yellow, golden sun catchers
swimming, clean bathing	orange, tangerine
sandy, stony, dry	many, bountiful, crisp
squeaky, pleasureable	accents of spectacular colors to the
water soaked, sun enriched	blue sky
SNOW	**SPRING**
beautiful, wonderful	reversed autumn
cool, clean, fresh	beginning of life, metamorphic
cold, pure, crisp	birth of plants
tingling, frosty	budding, sprouting, blooming
entertaining, playful	blossomy, sweet smelling
energizing, exhilarating	fresh, new, ongoing
thick, fluffy, cottony	flourishing

ANSWERS

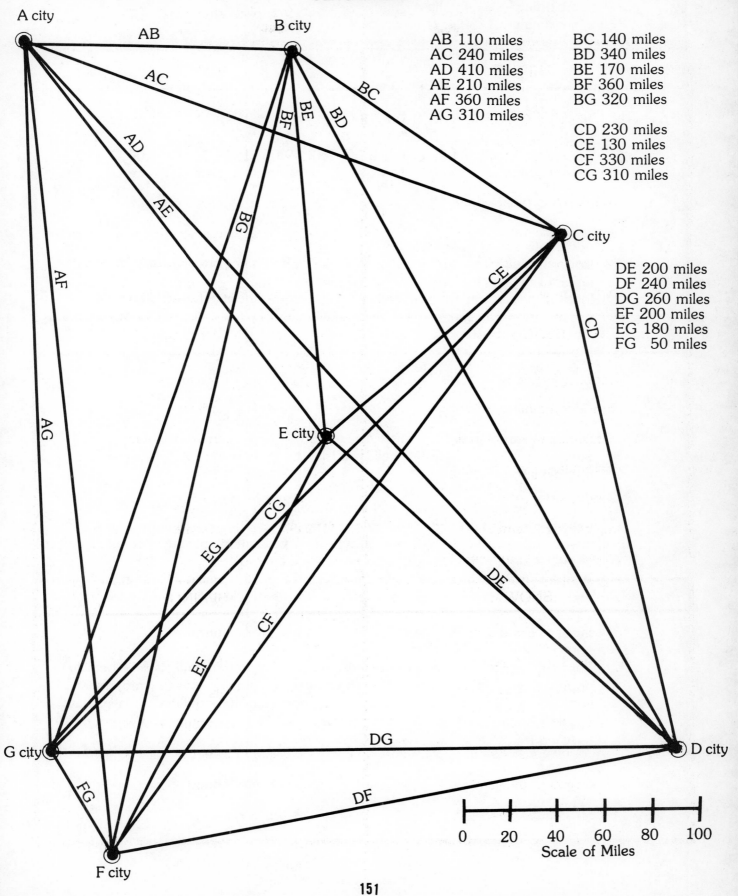

AB 110 miles
AC 240 miles
AD 410 miles
AE 210 miles
AF 360 miles
AG 310 miles

BC 140 miles
BD 340 miles
BE 170 miles
BF 360 miles
BG 320 miles

CD 230 miles
CE 130 miles
CF 330 miles
CG 310 miles

DE 200 miles
DF 240 miles
DG 260 miles
EF 200 miles
EG 180 miles
FG 50 miles

Scale of Miles
0   20   40   60   80   100

Measuring Perimeters, pages 20, 21
1. approximately 2600 miles
2. approximately 2050 miles
3. approximately 1450 miles

Figuring the Time..., pages 22, 23
3. three
4. 10:00, 4:00, 8:00, 3:00, 1:00, 12:00
5. 9:00, 7:00, 9:00, 12:00, 5:00, 10:00
6. 5:00, 3:00, 1:00, 9:00, 11:00, 3:00, 1:00, 9:00, 1:00, 11:00, 1:00, 12:00

Do You Know Your Atlas? pages 24, 25
1. similar to the following "A resource book of maps with other information about different regions in the world"
2. location places; capitals; time zones; flags; air distances between places; lakes; oceans; mountains; rivers of the world; climates of places; vegetation of places; etc.
3. Mt. Everest, Nepal
4. Nile in Africa
5. 4,969 miles
6. 7:00
7. Spain 40° N and 4°W   Michigan 44°N and 85°W
   Denmark 56°N and 10°E   Prague 50°N and 14°E
8. Moloka and Lanai (Hawaii), Falkland Islands, Iceland
9. approximately 300 miles
10. approximately 550 miles
11. latitude between 42° and 32°N—warm; big state (240 miles by 720 miles); heavily populated; high mountains; tourism; capital, Sacramento; deserts; lowest point in North America; (If atlas has vegetation, product, or resource maps, student may come up with more answers.)
12. Wintery because the angle of Northern Hemisphere is towards the sun right now and the Southern Hemisphere is away. Also the Falklands are quite far from equator, 52°S.
13. flying in the air, boating, etc.
14. approximately 14,400 miles
15. Possible answers: Montana is colder, bigger, has mountains, is less heavily populated, has Indians, etc. Mississippi is warmer, smaller, has few mountains, but has everglades and a big river, and is more heavily populated. (If atlas has vegetation, product, or resource maps, student may come up with more answers.)

	Australia	Brazil	Canada	Egypt	France	India	Iran	Japan	Mexico	New Zealand	South Africa	U.S.	Special Notes
A	X	X	X	14	17	X	X	X	X	X	★	X	
B	X	15	16	X	X	X	X	X	★	X	X	16	
C	X	★	16	X	X	X	X	X	16	X	X	16	
D	★	X	X	X	X	X	X	13	X	13	X	X	
E	X	X	16	X	X	X	X	X	16	X	X	★	she
F	X	16	★	X	X	X	X	X	X	X	X	16	
G	X	X	X	12	X	12	★	X	X	X	X	X	
H	X	X	X	X	★	X	X	X	X	X	17	X	
I	X	X	16	X	X	X	X	★	X	X	X	X	
J	13	X	14	X	X	X	X	14	X	★	14	X	
K	13	14	X	★	X	14	X	X	14	14	14	X	
L	X	X	X	X	14	★	X	14	X	X	X	14	

*Interpretation of matrix is on page 154.

Answers:
A—	South Africa	G—	Iran
B—	Mexico	H—	France
C—	Brazil	I—	Japan
D—	Australia	J—	New Zealand
E—	USA	K—	Egypt
F—	Canada	L—	India

Below is one possible way of deriving at a solution; however, it is not necessary to go in the order as was done here to solve the puzzle.

Numbers 1 through 12:	Researching an atlas, figure out all possible countries the agents could not be in and cross out on matrix. Some helpful suggestions: Number 2: Probably should use globe for accuracy in mileage. Number 5: May have to divide country's total square miles by its population to get population per square miles. After numbers 1 through 12 have been figured out, the only possibility for Iran is G.
Number 13:	Only three countries whose capitals begin with C are Australia, Egypt, and South Africa. By looking at the crossed out items on the matrix, D could only be Australia. In some way on matrix, it should be indicated all the other countries now that can not be D and all the agents that can not be in Australia. Indicate this by filling in squares with number that makes this clear. All future solutions are handled in same way. Answers are starred.
Number 14:	There is only one possiblity for K and that is Egypt, whose capital is Cairo, by the Nile Delta. That leaves only one possible agent for India—L and New Zealand—J.
Number 15:	B is either United States, Mexico, or Canada, because each has a large river that divides it from another agent's country. It's also established that B borders E, a she.
Number 16:	F also borders E. That automatically eliminates F as Brazil, which does not border another agent's country. So B, E, and G are the United States, Mexico, and Canada, and B and F both border E, so E has to be the United States. F can't be Mexico (established in #12), so must be Canada. That leaves B as Mexico. That leaves I in Japan and C in Brazil.
Number 17:	Agent G is Iran. Of the two countries left (France and S. Africa) France is the only one northwest of Iran. Thus, France is Agent H. That leaves S. Africa as A.
Number 18:	Extra clue to help out.

Almanac Questions, pages 44-46

The questions to go with these answers were devised with the intention that they should still be appropriate for use in future editions of these almanacs: *Reader's Digest Almanac; The World Almanac* by NEA; and the *Information Please Almanac*. However, a few of the answers will fluctuate with the yearly updating of these almanacs. These answers are denoted with astericks and should be updated accordingly by the teacher when appropriate.

1. James J. Blanchard *
2. $1000.00 *
3. 45
4. 1,148,000 kilowatts or
   1.148 megawats *
5. Yuri A. Gagarin
6. Iowa
7. State University of New York
8. 20013
9. Will vary with updating *
10. Richard Nixon
11. John Tyler
12. General John A. Wickham, Jr. *
13. 1835
14. Southeast Africa
15. July 4, 1776
16. *Rocky*
17. 240-258 square miles
18. varies with state student lives in
19. *Reader's Digest*
20. Texas besieged Alamo and declared
    independence.
21. right to speedy trial with witnesses
22. Ogden, Utah
23. deep
24. Richard Starkey
25. one of the following:
    United States, Canada, Iceland,
    Norway, Great Britian,
    Netherlands, Denmark,
    Belgium, Luxemburg, Portugal,
    France, Italy, Greece,
    West Germany, Spain, Turkey

26. $20.00 under 18 years old
    $35.00 over 18 years old
27. "Ring of Fire"
28. Greenland
29. 47th
30. Guadalupe Mountains National Park
    Big Bend National Park
31. Mountain State
32. Tracy Austin
33. 1593
34. 480-483 million miles
35. 36
36. varies according to student's birthday
37. 1,296
38. Washington
39. 36°N
40. About 64,000,000 miles
41. Archie Griffin
42. Ponce de León
43. 400 Maryland Ave., SW 20546
44. Will vary with updating. *
45. Flag Day
46. 60 Minutes *
47. O'Hare International
48. 14 *
49. Paul VI
50. Montreal

STATE X	STATE Y
1. less populated than Y (less county seats) 2. less rivers and lakes 3. cold part of year (latitude) 4. much smaller (see scale) 5. deserts 6. mountains (elevation high) 7. probably good state for snow skiing 8. bordered by four states 9. bordered by another country 10. probably a state attracted by tourists—sightseeing, a national park, snow skiing	1. more populated than X (more county seats) 2. more rivers and lakes 3. warm all year round (latitude) 4. much larger (see scale) 5. everglades 6. elevation low 7. bordered by three states 8. bordered on east by ocean 9. probably good state for most warm weather sports 10. probably a state attracted by tourists—warm weather and by ocean for water sports and fun

State Category Game, pages 99-105
Numbers correlate to state facts and are under categories in which they could fit.

Agriculture/Products: 1,3,20, 41, 43, 58, 66, 67, 69, 87, 92, 93

Climate: 9, 10, 22, 25, 34, 35, 51, 61, 72, 74, 76, 90, 94, 96

Entertainment/Recreation: 27, 28, 30, 31, 51, 64, 77, 78, 85, 95

Famous/Special: 12, 13, 15, 24, 27, 29, 33, 47, 48, 50, 53, 55, 73, 80, 84

History: 11, 24, 49, 60, 75, 86, 88

Industry: 2, 7, 17, 40, 44, 46, 65, 68, 79, 87

Inhabitants: 8, 23, 29, 56, 62, 91

Location: 16, 25, 52, 61, 89

Natural Resources: 7, 17, 39, 45, 79

Topography: 5, 6, 12, 18, 37, 38, 42, 59, 63, 71, 73, 77, 81, 82

Tourist Attractions: 12, 14, 19, 27, 28, 31, 72, 78, 80, 81, 83

Tradition: 4, 19, 57, 78

Vegetation: 21, 26, 36, 38, 42, 54, 71